CHRISTMAS CRAFTS FOR EVERYONE

CHRISTMAS CRAFTS FOR EVERYONE

EVELYN COSKEY

Illustrated by Roy Wallace

*Photographs unless otherwise indicated
are by Sid Dorris*

ABINGDON
Nashville

CHRISTMAS CRAFTS FOR EVERYONE

Copyright © 1976 by Abingdon

Library of Congress Cataloging in Publication Data

Coskey, Evelyn, 1932-
  Christmas crafts for everyone.
  Bibliography: p. 141
  Includes index.
  SUMMARY: Directions for making Advent and Christmas crafts from many lands.
  1. Christmas decorations—Juvenile literature. 2. Christmas—Juvenile literature. [1. Christmas decorations. 2. Handicraft] I. Title.
TT900.C4C67   745.59'41   76-4916

ISBN 0-687-07815-6

Photograph and directions for the crocheted Christmas tree ornaments courtesy of the National Cotton Council.

Jacket photograph of tree decorated with ornaments from this book was taken at Cheekwood Mansion courtesy of the Tennessee Botanical Gardens and Fine Arts Center, Inc. in Nashville, Tennessee.

MANUFACTURED BY THE PARTHENON PRESS AT NASHVILLE, TENNESSEE, UNITED STATES OF AMERICA

For Dr. Jozef Szczepkowski
who gave me Poland

ACKNOWLEDGMENTS

Without the help of a special group of people and agencies, this book could not have been written. I especially thank the following for their valuable assistance:

June Martin, Kanawha County Public Library in Charleston, West Virginia; The Library of Congress; The Santa Fe, New Mexico Public Library; The Pennyslvania State Library; The Janusz Bieniak Family of Warsaw, Poland; Maria Trapp, Stowe, Vermont; The Reverend Warren Thuston, pastor of the Church of the Trinity in St. Albans, West Virginia; Mrs. T. David Higgins; Mrs. Laura Wiik; Frau Hirschmann and Frau Rogeberg of Nürnburg's Noricama; Father Terry Linos; Theological Consultant Dr. W. Gordon Ross; Neil DiTeresa, Berea College Art Department in Berea, Kentucky; The Mexican Government Tourist Office; The Italian Tourist Office; The Hungarian Tourist Office; The Romanian Tourist Office; The German Tourist Office; The Austrian Tourist Office; The Danish Tourist Office; and The Swedish Tourist Office.

Special thanks to my mother, Mrs. C. E. Coskey, who served as a cat-sitter while I was in Europe working on the book, and to Juliette, for enduring it all.

CONTENTS

Contents

INTRODUCTION

Christmas observances are becoming similar the world over. There is still a distinct difference, however, between the European customs—in which Advent and the Christmas Crib are stressed—and the American ones. Objecting in ever-increasing numbers to the over-commercialization of our holiday, Americans are more and more turning to the European ways in order to bring Christmas back into its proper perspective: one in which Christ, above all, is emphasized. A major stumbling block has been a lack of adequate information on the making of European Christmas-related crafts.

This book provides high-interest, craft-oriented activities, many of which were researched in Europe and are not available in other American resources. These crafts have been tested for accuracy and can be used with children from grade five up. Unique and interesting material will make this a valuable book for teachers, public and school librarians, and workers with children, as well as the general reader.

WHY WE CELEBRATE CHRISTMAS

Why We Celebrate Christmas When We Do

Christmas is a holiday most of us have been celebrating for as long as we can remember. Nearly everyone knows something about it and what it means, but there is still a curtain of mystery hanging over the origins of the special day. This is because no one actually knows just when Jesus was born, or in fact just when Christians began to set aside a particular day to mark that momentous event.

During the early years of Christianity, there were many concerns that kept the minds of the believers on other things. For example, most of them were looking expectantly for an early return of Christ from heaven to judge the world and to rescue his followers from the pagan ways and the cruelty of the Roman Empire. They were thinking so earnestly of the future that it seldom occurred to them to look back and remember the events of the past. Only the Easter feast, honoring the Resurrection, had a regular place in the worship calendar. But then, every Sunday was a little celebration of the Resurrection.

As year after year after year went by, it became obvious that the Second Coming was not just around the corner, and all the while more and more men and women were joining the ranks of the Christians, coming from the population of the empire, folks who had become accustomed to keeping the boisterous pagan festivals. At first the church opposed every kind of merrymaking that smacked of paganism. But in time this attitude mellowed, and it came to be understood that the old habits went too deep and touched something very elemental in humankind. So the church wisely decided to take the processions and song and greenery and gaiety, and baptize them into the new life and make them a gift for the Babe who was born a King, and whose coming they wished to commemorate.

The most important pagan festivals had focused on the sun and the gods associated with it. Of course, from the very earliest times, people had noticed that the strength of the sun is greatly reduced during winter when the days are shorter and the weather is colder. The Roman Saturnalia and the Mithraic rites were designed to help the sun win out against the powers of darkness. Many of the elements of these celebrations were brought in and transformed to serve God whom the Christians knew as the powerful creator of the sun and the winter, and also of the fruits of the earth that the sun brought forth. But this God also had walked among men, beginning as a tiny baby. Who would not celebrate?

There was naturally some dispute about the proper date to be chosen, and not everyone agrees even to this day, but it was agreed that the time of the winter festival was fitting, for the darkness that had through the ages frightened and threatened to defeat the ancient pagans, had been forever defeated by the coming of the Christ Child.

Actually, it was not until A.D. 350 that December 25 was made the official date by Pope Julius I. With only a few minor setbacks, it has been going strong ever since. It has even attracted a whole cluster of other celebrations around it, until there is now an Advent season before Christmas, and twelve days of Christmas feasting.

16

Why We Celebrate Christmas

From Advent to Epiphany—A Calendar

November

November 14—St. Philip's Day. In homes of faithful members of the Eastern Orthodox Church, preparations are made for the start of Advent.

November 15—The first day of Advent for members of the Eastern Orthodox Church. This period is called the *Quadragesima*, or "Forty Days," of St. Philip. Another name is "Little Lent" because members of the church observe a period of fasting during Advent, although it is not as strict as Lent.

November 21—Feast of the Presentation of the Virgin Mary in the Temple (Eastern Orthodox).

November 29—Eve of St. Andrew's Day. In Poland, this celebration is a festive time for girls. They play fortune-telling games called *Andrzejki*—Andrew's Games—to discover who will find husbands during the coming year. Girls cut branches from a cherry tree and place it in water in a warm place. It is believed that if it blossoms by Christmas or New Year's, they will have a marriage proposal by the year's end.

November 30—St. Andrew's Day. The first day of Advent for Roman Catholics.

*Sunday following St. Andrew's Day—*The first day of Advent for Protestants and other Western churches.

December

December 4—St. Barbara's Day. Cherry branches are sold in many central European markets and are placed in water in a warm place on St. Barbara's Day. If they blossom by Christmas Eve, it is believed one will have good luck throughout the year. The branches are tended

17

by young girls who want husbands. If the branches flower on Christmas Eve, it is believed that the young girls will get their wishes. In Syria and Lebanon, the day is one of the most festive of the holiday season. In some areas, it resembles an American Halloween with boys going about in costumes and begging treats. In others, parties similar to those in America are held. An adult plays the role of St. Barbara. Afterward, the children are sent by parents to deliver gifts to the poor.

December 5—Eve of St. Nicholas' Day. In many parts of Europe, children set out special treats for St. Nicholas' horse. In Berchtesgaden, Germany, the *Butn'mandl Laufen*—strange, pagan creatures dressed in straw or fur, carrying whips, and with very loud bells around their waists—make their annual appearance in the St. Nicholas' Eve parade. Afterward, they go about whipping almost anyone they can catch and sometimes kissing the women.

December 6—St. Nicholas' Day. Many European children get their Christmas gifts on this day. Parades and other special activities are held.

December 8—Feast of the Immaculate Conception. An important feast day for all Roman Catholics. In some parts of Latin America the day equals—or surpasses—Christmas or Easter.

December 12—Feast Day of the Virgin of Guadalupe in Mexico. Generally a festive affair with fairs and other activities, but for some it is a deeply penitent time; they make their way on their knees to the local church named in honor of the Virgin.

December 13—St. Lucia's Day. The day marks the beginning of the Christmas season in Scandinavia. In Sweden, the oldest daughter in the family dresses as St. Lucia and, very early in the morning, serves coffee and special Lucia buns to members of the family while they are still in bed. In many parts of Sweden, Lucia queens are chosen. A national one is crowned at Skansen, an outdoor folk museum in Stockholm. In Hungary, it is the most important winter holiday for women. In the old days, all work was forbidden for them, especially spinning. St. Lucia would punish any woman who spun on her day. Women would dress in white with masks on their faces, and go about the villages inspecting the conduct of the children. In western Hungary, the fate of the chickens was decided for the coming year by small boys going about the villages reciting verses in honor of the saint and urging her to help the chickens lay many eggs. They were rewarded with small gifts. The men began at this time to make Lucy stools. They took them to Midnight Mass on Christmas Eve and used them to identify the village witches.

December 16-24—The Nine Days Before Christmas. In Roman Catholic countries, each day represents one of the months Mary carried the Holy Infant. Special religious ceremonies are held honoring the Holy Family. In Mexico, it is the time of the *Posadas*, dramas reenacting the Holy Family's search for lodgings. In Central and South America, *Novenas*, nine-day worship periods, are held in honor of the Holy Child. In Central Europe, the period is called the "Golden Days." It is a festive time with special masses held before dawn each day and worship services after dark each night.

December 24—Christmas Eve. Although Roman Catholics are no longer required by the church to maintain a fast, many continue to do so as a matter of personal preference. In many countries, though little food is eaten on Christmas Eve day, a great deal is being cooked. For the Polish people, one of the most festive meals of the year comes at the *Wigilia*, or Christmas Vigil, while the French and others feast after attending Midnight Mass. This is the night of the Christmas Vigil, one of the most important in the year. Many Catholics go to confession in preparation for receiving Holy Communion at Mass that night. In some countries, especially in the Germanic ones, Christmas Eve is the time for family gift-giving. The afternoon may be devoted to trimming the Christmas tree, usually by the parents and behind closed doors. The Polish Wigilia is a memorable experience. All day the women of the family have been cooking while the younger members have been busy decorating the Christmas tree and taking care of last-minute chores. Someone goes to the church for the *Oplatek*. Few have eaten during the day, so all look forward eagerly to the appearance of the first star—the signal for the festive meal to begin. Guests are considered a blessing at the Wigilia meal. An old Polish proverb says *Gość w domu, Bóg w domu,* or "A guest in the home is God in the home." Many members of the family gather for the meal. The most important part of the supper comes before any food is placed on the table. This is the sharing of the Oplatek, a thin white wafer embossed with the Nativity scene and made in the convents. It is a reminder of our daily bread and of the Bread of Life. Each person present is given one of the wafers, then the ceremony begins. The father and mother, facing one another and each holding an Oplatek, warmly embrace and express their love for the other. Each breaks off and eats a bit of the other's Oplatek. This ceremony is repeated all around the table with each person breaking off and sharing a bit of the other's wafer while expressing mutual love and concern. Then the actual meal begins. Poles regard the Oplatek as so important that it is mailed to relatives or close friends unable to attend the Wigilia. In Roman Catholic countries, the Midnight Mass is the center of the holiday festivities and marks the end of the long Advent season. It is often followed by an elaborate meal, the famous Réveillon in France which always concludes with the chocolate-covered *Bûche de*

Nöel, a cake Yule log. In Latin America, the Mass is called the *Missa de Gallo*, the "Mass of the Cock," because the cock begins his daily crowing shortly afterward. Protestant practices vary from church to church. For many, a midnight service is held, often a Communion service, with no service on Christmas Day. The Anglicans usually have both. The Sunday before Christmas is traditionally one of the major services of the Protestant church year with many attending church services on that day but not on Christmas Eve or Christmas Day. In Sweden the Christmas service is held at five o'clock on Christmas morning. The Eastern Orthodox celebration is distinctly different from the Roman Catholic and Protestant services because members of this church celebrate not only the birth of Jesus and the coming of the shepherds to the cave, but the arrival of the Wise Men as well. All the gospel accounts concerning these things are part of the Byzantine liturgy at Christmas. One theme of the religious service on Christmas Eve tells of Joseph's doubts concerning Mary's child, a point not often emphasized in the other churches. Another theme depicts Mary as reversing the mistake which Eve made.

December 25—Christmas Day. Roman Catholics who were unable to attend Midnight Mass attend another of the Masses on Christmas Day. Most Protestants have already attended their services, as have members of the Eastern Orthodox faith. When church services are over, the remainder of the day is a family time. Those who have not opened their gifts on Christmas Eve do so on Christmas Day, with small children getting their parents up at the crack of dawn to see what Santa has brought. Protestants frequently have their major festive meal on Christmas Day, often with members of the family who live at some distance in attendance. Christmas Day marks the end of the holiday season for many nonliturgi-

21

cal Protestants, but the season is by no means over for Roman Catholics, Anglicans, or members of the Eastern Orthodox Church. Roman Catholics and liturgical Protestants observe the week between Christmas and New Year's Day as an octave, a week-long liturgical observance of a major church feast. The last day is called the octave day. Included in the week are a number of special holidays.

December 26—St. Stephen's Day. St. Stephen's Day is a general holiday throughout Europe and the British Isles. Named for the apostle who was stoned to death for his beliefs, the meaning of the day varies from country to country. It is commonly accepted as the Second Day of Christmas. In England, this day is known as Boxing Day. Originally this was almost as important as Christmas Day itself because it was on this day that the village priest would open the "poor box" at the church and distribute the money to the needy. Gradually it came to be the custom to give Christmas boxes to servants and to those who performed public services—tradesmen, postmen, newsboys, and others in similar work. They go about with boxes, hoping to collect some extra money. In Roman Catholic countries, St. Stephen's Day has a special significance in agricultural areas. Since St. Stephen is the patron saint of horses, it is on his day that the Blessing of the Horses is held.

December 27—St. John's Day. Roman Catholics hold a wine-blessing ceremony, remembering St. John's successful attempt to stop an enemy who tried to kill him with poisoned wine.

December 28—Holy Innocents' Day. A feast in memory of the slaughter of babies by King Herod. Since the Middle Ages, it has been the custom for schoolboys to choose a boy bishop for the day. The practice is still observed in many places.

December 31—St. Sylvester's Day. St. Sylvester, a pope,

baptized Constantine the Great, bringing about a new era in Christianity. St. Sylvester's Day is also New Year's Eve, and some Protestants observe Watch Night services.

January

January 1—New Year's Day. A holy day of obligation for Roman Catholics. The Mass commemorates the Circumcision of the Infant Jesus and the octave day of Christmas. It is St. Basil's Day in the Eastern Orthodox Church and a major holiday. The first person to enter the house in the new year is considered very important. The dinner table is richly laden on New Year's Day since this signifies an abundance of food throughout the year.

January 6—Epiphany. The Feast of the Three Kings for Roman Catholics, Anglicans, and many other Western churches. Advent ends for members of the Eastern Orthodox Church on this day with the commemoration of the Baptism of Jesus. In many areas, a cross is thrown into a body of water and several worshipers go after it, no matter what the weather. The one who retrieves the cross is specially blessed.

THE DAYS BEFORE
CHRISTMAS

ADVENT WREATHS

Advent wreaths may take many forms. The one you choose will depend on the materials you can most easily obtain, your skills, and personal preference. Some wreaths can be made with materials already in the house or readily available, while others require more specialized materials. Most Advent wreaths require a substantial quantity of evergreen twigs. Be sure that the twigs are from a type of evergreen which does not shed its needles too readily since the wreath will be in use for at least four full weeks. Avoid hemlocks or spruces which shed their needles quickly.

The Advent wreath is trimmed with ribbon and four candles. Each candle has its own name, but the colors used usually depend on church or local custom. Roman Catholic and Episcopal churches often use a pink or rose candle on the Third Sunday in Advent. This is called Gaudete Sunday and is an especially joyful time. These churches also often use a fifth candle, white and larger than the others, which is called the Christ Candle and is put into the center of the wreath on Christmas Eve.

During the evening meal or family devotions in the first

24

week of Advent, the first candle, the Candle of Prophecy, is lighted and left burning until the period is over. The person who lights the candle is chosen by the family or the group. A person with a name which comes from John is often selected because it was John who first called Jesus the light of the world.

During the second week both the Candle of Prophecy and the second candle, the Candle of Bethlehem, are lighted. In the third week of Advent, the Shepherds' Candle is lighted along with the first two. During the fourth week of Advent the Angels' Candle is added to the lighting ceremony. If a fifth candle is used, it is added to the wreath on Christmas Eve and lighted with particular ceremony by someone considered worthy of that special honor.

Traditionally, the head of the household repeats a prayer as each candle is lighted. This ceremony can work well even if the group is not a family. A leader can be selected.

Newspaper-Based Advent Wreath (Basic Rule)

This type of Advent wreath is a very popular one in Scandinavia. It is easy to make and uses materials commonly found in the house. You may use it as a table or ceiling wreath by making simple adjustments in its construction.

Materials

Stiff wire long enough to form a circle the desired size (a wire clothes hanger is good, or the wire used to bind newspapers)

Old newspapers—allow at least two complete papers for each wreath, depending on their thickness

Spool of fine flexible wire

Evergreen twigs

4 long nails that extend 1 inch above surface of the wreath

Ribbon about 1½ inches wide to wrap around the wreath—allow 1½ yards for a table wreath

Fern pins (optional)

8 yards narrower ribbon in the same color as above for hanging wreath (optional)

4 candles 6- or 7-inches long, the same color as the ribbon (unless otherwise specified by church custom)

Method

1–Shape the wire into a circle the size you want your wreath. Twist the ends together.

2–Form the newspaper into a roll around the frame to obtain the desired thickness.

3–Anchor the newspaper to the frame with fine wire. Do not skimp on the wire. You will need it around the wreath later on. Twist wire ends together and tuck into paper.

4–Soak the newspaper-wrapped wreath frame in water until the newspapers are thoroughly wet. This helps keep the twigs fresh once they are in place.

5–Tie the twigs together in small bunches with fine wire. Using more wire, fasten the bunches in place, tying them to the wire holding the newspaper in place.

6–When you have completely covered the frame with evergreen twigs, force the nails through the wreath at even intervals from the underside. They will form the candleholders.

7–Wrap the wreath, in an even spiral, with the wide ribbon. You should have one band of ribbon between each candleholder. Secure the ends of the ribbon with pins or sew them firmly.

8–To hang the wreath, cut the narrow ribbon into four even sections. Sew these to the wider ribbon on the underside of the wreath at even intervals between the candleholders. Gather ends at the top.

9–Remove the nails and heat. Insert into the bottom of each candle. Replace nail in wreath and fit candle in place. If necessary, brace with fern pins. Light in the regular Advent order.

Styrofoam-Based Advent Wreath

A craft supply shop usually carries a 14-inch styrofoam base for this simple wreath.

1–Mark the places where you want the candles to go with a pencil. Position the circles at an even distance from the center and outer edge.

2–With a sharp knife, cut out the circles, making them a tiny bit smaller than marked. Cut through the bottom of the wreath to form holders for the four main candles.

3–Secure the candles using fern pins or invisible hairpins.

4–Fasten evergreen twigs around each candle.

5–Fill in any exposed surface of the styrofoam form with more evergreen twigs, fastening them in place with pins.

6–If the wreath is to be hung, cover the bottom of the wreath with greenery.

7–Make a large bow from one yard of wide ribbon and attach it to the wreath.

8–To hang the wreath, cut 8 yards of ribbon into four equal parts. Fasten them securely to the underside of the wreath and gather the ends together at the top.

9–For a table wreath, put the finished wreath on a tray in the center of the table. On Christmas Eve place a tall white candle in the center of the wreath.

The Days Before Christmas

Wire Frame Advent Wreath

This type of wreath is also quite easy to do. It may be used for hanging on the door; just leave off the ribbons and candles and trim in any way you like. Twelve- or fourteen-inch wreath frames and spagnum moss or Oasis can be bought at little cost in most craft shops or floral supply stores.

1–Purchase a wreath frame that is rounded on top and hollow inside. Fill the hollow with moss or Oasis and wrap with fine wire to hold it in place.

2–Soak the wreath in water until the moss or Oasis has absorbed as much moisture as possible. Drain off excess.

3–Wrap the wreath in aluminum foil or plastic wrap. If you use plastic wrap, tape it in place if necessary.

4–Insert the nails as in Basic Rule.

5–Cut evergreen into desired lengths and sharpen the ends with a knife.

6–Insert the twigs until you have covered the entire form.

7–Decorate the wreath with ribbon and put the candles in place.

Norwegian Straw Advent Wreath

These straw Advent wreaths are different because evergreens are not used. They are commonly seen in Norwegian shops during the Advent season. Since these wreaths require long lengths of straw, the materials for making them may be a bit difficult to find in many areas.

1–Form a piece of stiff wire into a circle and twist the ends together to fasten.

2–Form a hoop of straw by wrapping the circle with long pieces of straw. Bind the straw in place with fine wire or twine at 1-inch intervals.

29

3–Push four long nails through the straw at even intervals centering them between the inner and outer edges, to form the candleholders.

4–Wrap wide red ribbon around the wreath in an even spiral, with one loop between each spike. Sew or pin the ends of the ribbon firmly in place.

5–To hang the wreath attach narrow ribbons for hanging. Anchor them firmly to the spiraled ribbon. Gather the upper ends together and attach to fastener.

6–Put a red candle on each spike as in Basic Rule.

Baked Advent Wreath

For a different kind of holiday decoration, use a baked Danish Advent wreath made from strips of braided dough and decorated with candles, candied fruit or nuts, and greenery. For the recipe for this Advent wreath see page 85.

ADVENT CALENDARS

Advent calendars have been popular in Europe for many years and are gaining favor in America. There is a wide variety of calendars. Some are flat, others are three-dimensional with figures that stand out, and still others are

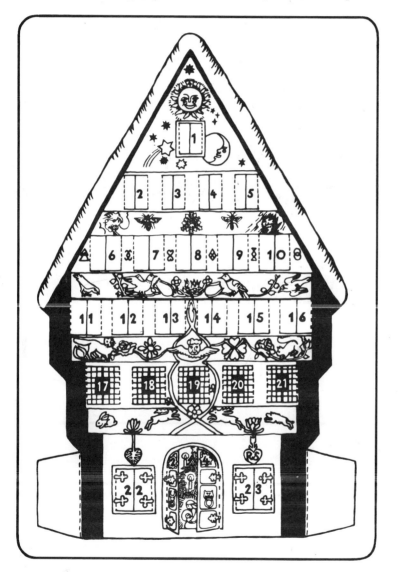

designed to fold into different shapes. Most have twenty-four or twenty-five windows with a picture hidden under each for the pre-Christmas days in December, and a picture of the Nativity under the last window.

In some calendars, the windows are simply cut at random, putting them wherever you please, with—or without—any relationship to the scene. In other calendars, the windows are squares forming a background for the picture; with these calendars, the windows are not numbered consecutively, and having to search for the next number adds to the fun. Still another type of Advent calendar, especially intended for small children, uses no windows at all; hooks are used and a little gift is hung on each one. Every day of Advent, the child has a present to open.

Making an Advent Calendar

Advent calendars are easy to make—especially since there are so few rules to follow. About all you need is a large picture of some kind with twenty-four or twenty-five smaller pictures, including a picture of the Nativity.

For best results, Advent calendars should be at least 9 inches by 12 inches, although they can be much larger. If you enjoy painting, you might like to make your own scene—perhaps it would be fun to make an Advent calendar showing the street on which you live—or you can use a picture from some other source. A large, jolly Santa or a Christmas tree would make a good secular calendar. For a religious one, you might get a Sunday school picture to use for the background, or you could make a large house with twenty-four windows and a door. Have an appropriate Bible verse behind the windows, with a Nativity scene behind the door. Another idea would be to make an Advent calendar featuring a Jacob's Ladder.

The Days Before Christmas

Materials

A large picture mounted on lightweight cardboard for the
  front of the calendar
23 or 24 small pictures to go behind the windows (used
  Christmas cards are an excellent source).
A picture of the Nativity, slightly larger than the others
Thin paper for the backing cut the same size as your
  picture
An X-acto knife or some other knife with a sharp point
Household white glue
Glitter, if desired

Method

1–Mark the front picture to show where the windows will
  be. You may locate them to correspond to objects in
  the pictures—actual windows, doors, in a chimney,
  behind a sun or moon,—or simply at random, any-
  where in the picture. Plan a large window for the last
  day on the calendar. Locate it in the center of the
  picture. Lightly mark the outlines of the windows with
  a ruler and pencil.
2–Using a ruler and the knife, cut through the marked
  outlines on the top, bottom and *one* side. On the fourth
  side, cut part-way through the cardboard so that the
  window will fold outward when it is opened. Do *not*
  open the windows.
3–Select small pictures to go behind the windows. They do
  not have to have any relationship to the scene, but it is
  better if they do. A picture of a small candle would be
  appropriate behind a church window, or a kitten
  playing would be good behind the window of a house.
  The Nativity scene should be the largest picture.
4–Cut the pictures a bit larger than the window openings.

33

Put a thin line of white glue around the edges of the pictures and glue them in place behind the windows. Try to center them so that the pictures will be directly behind the windows.

5–When all of the pictures are in place, put a thin line of glue around the edges of the backing paper and press it in place over the back of the calendar.

6–If desired, decorate by painting parts of the picture with white glue, then sprinkling with glitter. Shake off the excess.

A LUCIA CELEBRATION

If you are looking for something different to do at holiday time, you might want to have your own Lucia celebration on the thirteenth of December.

The Lucia Crown

The traditional Lucia crown is made of seven 5½-inch white candles in little holders attached to a inch-wide metal band decorated with evergreens.

To make a simple crown, cut an inch-wide band of lightweight cardboard long enough to fit around your head, then overlap an inch. Fasten the ends together with staples. Cut candles from white construction paper and staple to the band. Paint or crayon in the flame. Trim the crown with real evergreen twigs.

The Lucia Robe

The Lucia robes sold in Swedish stores look very much like white cotton nightgowns or like the simple robes worn by children's choirs. If you have a plain white nightgown, you may use it for your Lucia robe. If you need to make your own, you can do it very easily from an old bedsheet.

To make a robe, cut as shown. Sew the side seams, hem the bottoms of the sleeves and the neck. Turn a hem in the bottom edge of the robe. Use a long length of wide red ribbon for the belt.

If you want to have girl attendants for Lucia, make their robes in the same way. Make simple headdresses from wide silver Christmas tree garlanding cut to fit around their heads. Staple or sew the ends together. Belts are made from the same garlanding, cut to come about halfway down the front of the skirt.

Lucia Buns

Lucia buns are made in many shapes, the most popular being *Lussekatter*, or "Lucia cats." See page 88 for a recipe for these sweet buns and instructions on making the various shapes.

THE CHRISTMAS CRIB

For many families, the crèche is the central part of Christmas. A representation of the Nativity may be as simple or as elaborate as you care to make it.

Perhaps you will prefer to make the stable and the background, but buy the figures. Variety stores often carry attractive ones, frequently imported from factories in Italy or Germany, and usually at relatively little cost. This may be a good idea if members of your family or group are very young or just not artistic.

Some people like to collect figures for their crèches as they travel. It is exciting to search for appropriate figures in faraway places. It is also nice to pass crèche figures along from generation to generation. The slight difference in size and type will simply add to the charm of your scene.

It is important to determine the purpose of your crèche. Is it to be for your immediate family? To give to a shut-in? For the outside of your church? If the crèche becomes a very personalized part of your Christmas so much the better; it should express how *you* feel about the birth of Jesus.

As you plan your crèche, consider:

1–How much space is available for your crèche? This will

determine how large a set you will have and the size of the figures in it.

2–How much time do you have to devote to the construction?

3–Is this to be a group project? If so, it can be far more elaborate than one to which you can devote only a few hours.

4–How old are the members of your group? Very young children need something extremely simple, while older children or adults might enjoy the challenge of making an elaborate crèche.

5–Where do you live? Are natural materials, such as moss and rocks, available?

6–What skills are available? A small child who is clever at soap-carving might do the sheep while another child who knits or crochets could clothe the figures. An adult who likes to work with wood could make the stable.

7–In certain situations you might make the whole crèche in a year; in the home or church it might be a project to spread out over a period of years.

A CHRISTMAS CARD CRÈCHE

Since it folds flat for storage, this crèche makes an ideal gift for a shut-in, especially one who lives in a nursing home with little room for personal possessions. It would also be good in a very small apartment. A Christmas card crèche is easily made. It is an appropriate Advent project for an elementary class in school or church or a Scout troop.

If the crèche is to be a gift, design or buy an envelope to fit it. Also enclose directions for setting up the crèche. For more information, see Margaret Perry's *Christmas Card Magic*.

Materials

Lightweight cardboard, 12 inches by 18 inches

Additional pieces of brown construction paper or lightweight cardboard

Used Christmas cards (you may need to search through quite a few to find the kinds and sizes of figures you need)

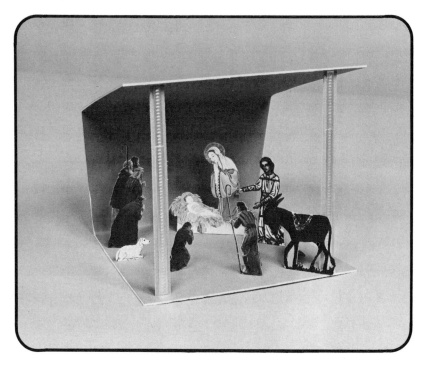

Method

1–Following the diagram, cut the stable from lightweight cardboard.

2–Using a pencil and ruler, lightly mark dotted lines on the outside of the cardboard. Fold along these lines, using the ruler, to get even folds. The floor is 7 inches from front to back, then the cardboard is bent up to form the back wall, which is 4½ inches high. The second fold brings the roof forward for 6½ inches.

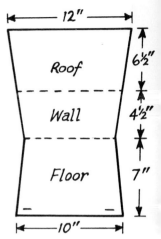

3—Make pillars from strips of cardboard cut 8 inches by ½ inch. If desired, decorate them with vertical designs cut from Christmas cards or paint on your own designs.

4—Glue each pillar in place inside the roof, placing each edge 1½ inches from the side and ½ inch from the front edge of the roof.

5—On the floor of the crèche, make ½ inch slits, ½ inch from each side and ½ inch from the front edge.

6—Bend the lower ½ inch of each pillar to the back. Slip the folded end into one of the slits in the floor.

7—Cut the figures you plan to use from Christmas cards.

8—Make the bases for each figure from matching construction paper by cutting a strip ¼ inch wide and the height of the figure.

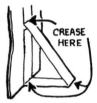

9—Glue a portion of the strip to the figure as shown. Fold the remainder of the strip into three equal sections. Crease and glue as shown.

10—Arrange the standing figures as desired in your crèche. To fold for storage, put the base behind the figure.

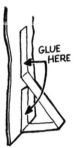

BUILDING A CRÈCHE

Families or groups who have a great deal of time and who enjoy working together may want to make an elaborate European-style crèche. The size of your crèche figures and the space, materials, and time available will determine the style and character of the project. Crèches of this kind must be planned months in advance, preferably well before the first frost. In her excellent book *Cradling the Christ Child*, Liselotte Nold gives detailed instructions for constructing a crèche of this type. Some of her suggestions follow here.

The Figures

Before you actually begin, read the second chapter of the Gospel of Luke, then reread it to those who will be working on the crèche. By the time you have finished, you will discover that the gospel writer has told you exactly how to build the crèche.

Figures are available in a wide variety of sizes, styles, and prices. There are expensive ones that are true works of art, and others, more moderately priced, which can be very attractively used. The aim is to make an appropriate representation of the Nativity in which to set your figures.

You must assemble your figures before you start the actual building of the crèche since their size determines the proportion of the scene. The stable must be large enough to hold the Holy Family, but not so large that they look lost inside. If you plan to have stairs leading to the manger, they should be wide enough for the figures to fit on. The proportions of the figures determine not only the size of the buildings but also the types of plants you will use.

The Base

A tabletop about 3 feet by 5 feet makes a practical base for the crèche. If you buy something for a base, consider getting a piece of low-grade plywood. Since it will be completely covered, minor imperfections in the wood are of no consequence.

Ideally, the base should have a low border around it. Lathing or other thin wood at least 1 inch wider than your base can be easily fastened in place. You might paint the border dark green, dark gray, or brown before nailing it into place.

The Christmas Crib

Soak old newspapers in water, then roll and shape them to form the base for the landscape. Pieces of firewood will also work well if you can get them easily.

After the base has been built, use florist's clay to anchor the plants and figures.

The Stable

The stable should be built into the base. You might decide to construct a cave instead of a stable to shelter the Holy Family. In part, local custom will determine your choice; in part, it will be matter of personal preference.

If you choose to build an ordinary stable, follow the style of architecture in your neighborhood. You will need to make a large opening for the door so that the viewers as well as the characters in the story can see into the stable. You will want to have quantities of staw inside your crèche. To fireproof your crèche wet the straw with a standard formula used for Christmas trees. Combine 4 ounces of boric acid and 1 gallon of water. (A blender speeds this process.) Add 9 ounces of borax. Dip straw into the solution in a tub and shake off the excess. Let the straw dry. The mixture will not affect its appearance. The stable may also contain implements and utensils—perhaps a rake, a lantern, or a pair of boots for the farmer. Use these items to emphasize the fact that it is a stable, but not if you find that they distract from the overall effect.

The stable may be painted in any way you wish, but it should not look new. If you want your stable to have a weatherbeaten look, use dried moss cut into small pieces. (Moss is most easily cut with a pair of old scissors.) Then put the moss through a sieve. Brush the surfaces of the stable with glue, then sprinkle with moss dust. If you prefer, sawdust may be used to obtain a similar weathered effect.

41

If you have a skilled woodworker in your group, the stable can be fairly elaborate, but a painted cardboard box with the flaps cut off will do very well. If someone in your group is an especially skilled craftsman, you might like to add some houses along with a village street.

In Austria, the villagers and farm folk often construct crèches to resemble their own regions. Nold suggests the use of homey details such as woodpiles, flowerpots, birdhouses, and the like. You might want to add flower or vegetable gardens to your crèche.

If you desire to use the natural shelter or cave, you might want to construct a cliff in your crèche with the cave underneath. Then you may decide to build a shed or lean-to in the cave with pieces of wood. Here again, use moss and grasses for a natural, weathered look. Keep your eye open for roots and stones the right size and shape to add to your crèche.

You may also use a small cardboard box, with the flaps trimmed off, turned on its side for the base of the cave. Pack moss and small rocks around it until you have achieved the proper effect.

The Landscape

Once the stable has been built, plan the landscape to surround it. You may want smooth, flat meadows, or you may want sharp, rocky hills. The best material for a rolling meadow is firm, green moss. It should be carefully cleaned and each piece soaked in water before it is put into place.

Natural materials such as moss and gravel are helpful in building a crèche of this type. Your work will be easier if you have a large supply of moss. Before using the moss, soak it in water for a short time. This will keep it fresh longer and make it easier to handle. The moss will be used to fill in gaps and holes between the raised portions of the base. It also makes a good covering for the entire surface. In addition, moss can be used to make building materials look weatherbeaten. It can be kept and used again the following year.

Hills can be shaped from newspapers rolled and soaked in water. These may also be covered with moss. A jagged appearance may be achieved by using rocks and stones or pieces of wood.

Roots are very useful in building a crèche since they have many interesting and unusual shapes which suggest trees, shrubs, or vines. Arrange these in your landscape in a way that reflects the character of your area. Dried flowers also make effective shrubs and bushes.

You can prepare dried flowers yourself by selecting suitable ones from the garden in late fall. Pull them up by the roots, shaking off the dirt, then wash and hang to dry.

Another way to obtain trees and shrubs for your

Berea College, 1974

Cornshuck crèche

landscape is to dig small plants or seedlings from the yard, placing them in the scene with their roots in thick, wet moss. To make some of your trees or bushes "bloom," glue little dried flowerets—the kind that can be purchased in many gift and flower shops—here and there along the branches.

Many European crèche builders use real flowers, digging them up before the first frost and later placing them in the scene with their roots in wet moss. Flowers play an important part in the crèche. They are often found blooming near the Christ Child to symbolize joy over the birth of the Savior.

If you want to add roads or lanes for the Wise Men and the shepherds to travel, spread a mixture of sand and small gravel in the appropriate places.

To add lakes and streams to your landscape, use flat pieces of ordinary glass. Each piece should be carefully buried in the landscape with some soil beneath the glass. Bring the moss up to the edges to form the banks. Plant grass along the edges to give the appearance of reeds. A small bridge may be added. You can make a bridge by fastening a small piece of wood into the moss on either side of the glass. As a finishing touch to your landscape, you might want to build a fence using small twigs and sticks.

Lighting

If you have someone in your group who is skilled at working with lighting, you might illuminate your crèche. Candles are unsuitable. By clever use of electric lights, it is possible to set off groups of figures very effectively. For example, a small light can be hidden in the stable in such a way that the Holy Family is highlighted. Preferably, any lights used with the crèche should be yellow rather than white; they give a softer glow.

The Backdrop

Many crèches will be placed against a wall and need a backdrop of some kind. This can vary with your mood, your finances, and your creative talent. A blue bedsheet or a large piece of construction paper is one possibility. More artistic groups might prefer to make their own, using blue cloth with spatter-stencil stars or blue felt with silver stars.

Final Steps

The figures should be placed in groups, rarely one by one. According to the Gospel of Luke, people were in groups when they heard the news of the Savior's birth. Once the figures have been placed in the crèche, they may be attached to the base with clay so that they do not fall over. To keep the crèche fresh, it should be regularly sprinkled with water, taking care to water only the vegetation.

There are times when building the crèche will seem an unending chore. But, when the group comes together for its Christmas worship period and the crèche is lit up in a darkened room, the meaning of the Nativity will become clear for each member in a way it never has before. Each moment spent working on the crèche will seem an act of devotion, and the final result will be well worth the effort.

A LIVING NATIVITY SCENE

Many churches have living Nativity scenes outdoors at Christmas. To be effective, planning for such a display must begin months in advance, and this is doubly important if you expect to use animals as well as people. If proper attention is not given to the animals, you may have difficulties with your local humane society. Because individual circumstances vary greatly, only general guidelines can be given for setting up a living Nativity scene.

Planning

September is a good time to begin planning. A committee at the church should be in charge; for ease in handling matters, the group should consist of not more than ten to twelve people. A youth fellowship, a particular Sunday school class, or an organization within the church might form the committee. They can recruit more help if needed from outside the immediate group.

Particularly valuable in setting up a living Nativity scene will be several strong adults with the ability and tools for rough carpentering, a few persons who are imaginative as well as skilled in sewing, someone with a knowledge of lighting processes, at least one person with marked skill in stretching a dollar, and one or two persons with a knack for getting along with animals.

An absolute minimum of three hundred dollars should be allowed if you have never done a living Nativity scene before. If you have experience or access to some of the materials you will need, you may be able to get along with less. Even with this amount, you will have to depend quite heavily on donated materials *and* time. Part of the money allotted will be used to purchase animal feed.

The Stable

The stable should be rough. Scrap lumber can often be used in its construction. If you intend to dismantle the stable after Christmas and store it until the following year, take this into consideration when it is built. The stable should be sturdy enough to withstand the use it will get, but it should not be so solidly built that taking it down for storage will present problems. Be sure to consider the size of the church lot when you plan the stable, keeping it in proportion to the ground around it.

The Animals

Animals can be the trickiest part of the whole scene. They should be located as soon as possible after you decide to set up a living Nativity scene so that they can become acquainted with those who will be handling them; bringing them in ten minutes before the action begins is a sure way to guarantee chaos.

Depending on where you live, you may be able to find someone who will donate the use of necessary animals or you may have to pay for their services. The disposition of the animals is a major factor. A nervous animal can cause serious problems if he is frightened by traffic or passersby. By all means, have the person in charge of the animals get well acquainted with them as far ahead of time as is practical. A place will also have to be found at or near the church to shelter them. Food and water must be provided as well as a means of keeping them warm and clean.

Casting

This can be decided in a number of ways. One of the most practical solutions is to use volunteers. Young people home from college at Christmas often enjoy taking part in the pageant for at least one night. Since the costumes are the kind which fit almost anyone, this should present no serious problems.

Costuming

Many costumes can be improvised from sheets, remnants of cloth, and donated garments. Pictures of biblical garments can be found in most public libraries, and these may be used to provide guidelines for the seamstress. It should not be necessary to purchase expensive costumes.

The Performance

The duration of the performance is a strictly individual matter to be determined by the animals (how long you have them, their dispositions, and the cost of their use), the weather, and the amount of time the cast is willing to spend. Some churches merely have a one-night stand for two or three hours, while others put on the display nightly for the week between Christmas and New Year's.

The Christmas Crib

The decision to put on a pageant or a tableau is also a matter of individual preference. Some churches like the idea of a tableau since it is so much simpler, while others prefer to combine the living Nativity scene with a more elaborate pageant containing several scenes, background music (recorded or provided by the church choir or visiting choirs), and intricate lighting.

The Lighting

This again will be a matter of personal preference and circumstance. A simple spotlight will be very effective for a tableau—provided that care is taken that it does not shine directly in someone's eyes—while the pageant will require more complicated lighting. If you plan to have an outdoor pageant every year, the lighting equipment can be permanently fixed to trees in the vicinity and kept covered with plastic bags when not in use. This will save the trouble of taking it down and setting it up every year.

CHRISTMAS COMES FROM EVERYWHERE

AUSTRIAN FOIL ORNAMENTS

One of the favorite types of handmade Christmas tree ornaments in Austria are these simple foil decorations. They require no special equipment and may be made from easily obtained materials. The result is similar to the more difficult tin ornaments often seen in Mexico.

Materials

Heavy gold craft or decorator foil (available in craft shops)
Patterns (cookie cutters are ideal)
Knitting needle or dry ball-point pen
Paper punch

Method

1–Trace a pattern on the foil.
2–Cut out with old scissors.
3–Make a hanging hole with a paper punch.
4–Put the ornament face down on several thicknesses of newspaper.
5–Emboss whatever designs you want by drawing them

quite firmly on the back of the shape with a knitting needle or a dry ball-point pen.

6–Using a table knife, carefully smooth out any slight roughness or "curl" around the edges of the ornament.

7–To hang, use a partially unbent paper clip or a length of nylon line run through the hole.

GERMAN STAR

This attractive ornament can be a challenge to make, but the finished product is so pretty and durable, that it is well worth the trouble. For beginners the best material is strong, flexible paper. However, in Germany, where this ornament is a tradition, thin wooden strips are often used.

Materials

4 strips of paper ¾ inches wide and 24 inches long. Narrower strips may be used after the basic rule is mastered. It is important to cut the strips evenly, and it is easiest to work with two colors, 2 strips of each.

Method

1–Fold the strips in half and taper the ends as shown in figure 1.

51

2–Interlock the loops into a basket weave as shown also in figure 1.

3–Hold star so that one folded edge is on top at the righthand corner. Beginning at the top of the star, fold forward and crease the left front strip, and moving counterclockwise, fold forward the next two front strips. When folding the fourth strip, insert it into slot formed by the fold of the first strip. This locks the center of the star in place (see figure 2).

4–To make the points, start again at the top, using the strip on the right. Fold the strip to the back, making a diagonal crease at the base of the strip (see figure 3).

5–Fold forward, making a second diagonal crease, to form a triangle and to bring the strip to the front as shown in figure 4. Then fold toward front along center of triangle.

6–Work the end of this strip through the loop immediately beneath it (figure 5) and fold back to fasten in place. This makes one of the eight points. Fold, crease, and weave in each of the righthand strips in the same manner.

7–Turn star over and make four more points using the longer strips.

8–To make the standing points, bring four strips to upright position in the center. Take strip at top right, lift and turn under, around, and over in a counterclockwise direction to make a complete loop. Run the end of strip through the slot just beneath strip on the left (see figure 6). Pull to bring point into position. Repeat with each strip, until there are four standing points on each side of the star.

9–Trim ends close to folded star points. If these ends are pulled slightly for cutting, the clipped edge will retract into the point.

10–Insert ornament hook for hanging.

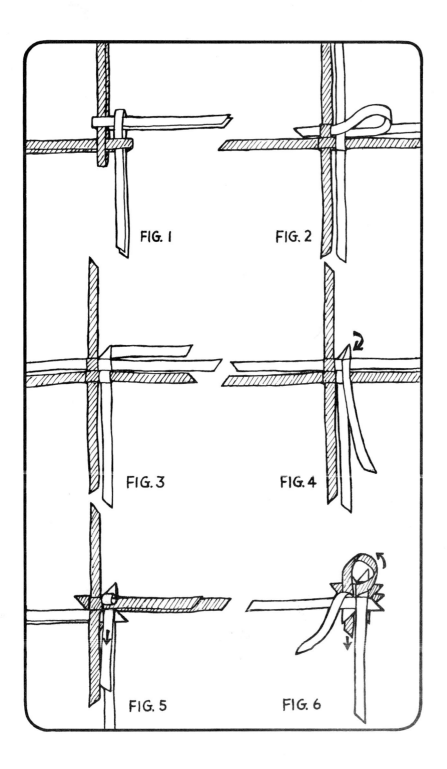

FIG. 1

FIG. 2

FIG. 3

FIG. 4

FIG. 5

FIG. 6

MEXICAN LANTERNS

Lanterns are popular, simple-to-make Christmas tree ornaments which are made in many countries, but they are special favorites in Mexico where they are used throughout the house. They may be made from plain construction paper or decorator foil.

Materials

Colored construction paper or foil
Rubber cement or paste

Method

1–Draw a rectangle the size you want your lantern to be. Cut it out and fold in half lengthwise.

54

2–On the wrong side, draw a margin the width desired for the top and bottom edge of the lantern. Fold each side outward along the line to make a crease. Open out these folds but leave the one dividing the paper in half lengthwise.

3–Starting at the fold, cut slits about ¼ to ½ inch apart, going to the second fold lines.

4–Decorate the upper and lower margins of the lantern, if desired.

5–Make a handle from a long, narrow strip of construction paper. Paste it in place.

6–Gently push the outer edges of the lantern toward the center.

7–Open out the rectangle. Fasten the short edges together with rubber cement or paste.

LUMINARIAS

Luminarias are sand-weighted paper bags with lighted candles inside them which are set along the edges of walks or rooftops. Though the custom is now observed in many parts of the world, luminarias originated in the American Southwest.

When the Spaniards first colonized New Mexico, they lacked the traditional festival lights. The people began, instead, making small bonfires of bright-burning piñon. These little fires on Christmas Eve lighted the processions to Midnight Mass and were placed in front of homes so the Christ Child could find his way.

In later years, bright wrappings were saved and fashioned into gay little paper lanterns, or *farolitos*, to decorate the patio or home for other festive occasions.

Finally, with the coming of paper bags and commercial

candles, New Mexicans once more improvised. This time they substituted candles in paper sacks for the bonfire luminarias. These were not lanterns, but symbolic little fires lit by those who believe the Christ Child wanders softly through the night and blesses all who set a guiding light.

Though the actual making of a luminaria is extremely simple, a display requires a large quantity of sand, which can be purchased from the building supply dealer or brought home from a seaside vacation. When you get your sand, be sure to store it in a dry place.

Luminarias are effective only if they are made in large numbers and placed quite close together—from one to three feet apart. If you are planning to outline the edges of a house roof, and a driveway as well, allow about five hundred luminarias.

If you are going to make many luminarias, plan to start at least three days before Christmas. Making them may be either a single or group project. Perhaps groups of Scouts would like to make them for use in their neighborhood or to brighten up a home for the elderly at Christmas.

A light wind would not prevent the use of luminarias, but do not attempt to use them when it is raining or snowing. It is perfectly acceptable to set the luminarias up on fallen snow.

On the afternoon of Christmas Eve, set the luminarias in place. Children should not be allowed to handle their placement on rooftops or other places where they might fall. The best time to light the luminarias is after dark on Christmas Eve. Since it takes time to light the luminarias, you might want to draft some friends or neighbors to help out with the job. Allow the candles to burn themselves out. Since they are anchored in sand, and the luminarias are not set close enough to each other to touch, there is little danger of fire from them. Keep small children away.

If you are the first in your neighborhood to try

luminarias, don't be surprised if others make them next year. And be prepared for extra traffic on your block, especially the second year.

Materials (for one luminaria)

One number 10 grocery paper sack
Votive candle or plumber's candle (regular candles are not suitable)
One cup sand

Method

1–Fold down the grocery sack until the top is only 2 to 3 inches high. Make the folds on the outside of the sack.
2–Put about a cupful of sand in the bottom of the sack.

3–Place a candle in the middle of the sand. Push it in just far enough to steady it.

4–To light the luminaria, use ordinary matches, long fireplace matches, or the lighted end of a dry stick.

PIÑATAS

Piñatas are an exciting feature of many Mexican holiday celebrations. Though they are mistakenly thought to be exclusively Mexican, the custom originated in the sixteenth century in the vineyards of Italy. During the fiesta to mark the end of the harvest, a clay pot was strung up on a tree, and blindfolded harvesters attempted to break it open with a stick. When this was accomplished, a shower of fruits and nuts fell to the ground.

The Spanish adopted the tradition embellishing their piñata pots with gaily colored designs. But it was in Mexico that the piñatas took on the characteristics which now make them world-famous.

The real Mexican piñatas are made with clay jars for their foundations, but very effective ones can be made from more readily available materials—balloons, newspapers, either flour-and-water paste or liquid laundry starch. Piñatas can be formed into many shapes such as animals or people as well as simple round balls. For more information, see *Piñatas* by Virginia Brock.

Materials (to be gathered *before* you start)

Large balloon, inflated and tied
Old newspapers

Christmas Comes from Everywhere

Liquid laundry starch or flour-and-water paste (one part
  flour to two parts of water, cooked or uncooked)
Rubber cement
Tissue paper, 20 inches by 30 inches
Small paintbrush
Hemp rope or heavyweight mailing twine

Method

1–Prepare the newspaper by tearing into strips of varying
   lengths 1 to 2 inches wide.
2–Dip the strips in starch or paste, wipe off the excess, and
   apply around the balloon. Place the first strip just
   below the area you plan to use for an opening. The
   opening should be near the top but should not
   interfere later with the hanging rope. Be sure to apply
   at least four layers of paper to support the form.
3–Place a dish towel under it to keep it in place while you
   work. A rinsing in cold water will remove the paste.
   (If you must leave your work at this point, put the
   form in a plastic bag and tie the top tightly.)
4–To decorate the piñata, it may be desirable to draw
   guidelines with chalk or crayon after the form is dry.
   The lines will be completely covered later.
5–When the form is thoroughly dried, deflate the balloon
   by snipping a hole in the exposed part. Cut away any
   part of the balloon that remains at the piñata opening.
6–Attach rope or twine in several loops to encircle the
   piñata from bottom to top. Masking tape will be
   helpful in attaching the rope. Make a stout loop at the
   top. The remaining part of the rope will be tied to this
   loop after the decoration is completed in order to
   suspend the piñata.
7–Make ruffles by folding a sheet of tissue paper crosswise

and cutting strips 3 inches wide. Fold each strip in half lengthwise. Cut fringe along the folded edge to within ½ inch of the cut. These slashes should be approximately ⅛ inch apart. Several ruffles can be made at one time by folding four or five strips together.

8–Unfold the ruffle with the folded side up, and use a small paintbrush to spread liquid starch or rubber cement (flour and water will not do) on one edge of the ruffle. Use small dabs at two- to three-inch intervals. Refold in the reverse direction. Press the edges together where you have applied starch or cement.

9–Apply starch or commercial paste to a small area of the piñata. Lay ruffling over the form as desired. Each new row should hide the pasting but show the ruffle of the preceding row. A large bowl makes a handy holder while pasting.

The ruffling can be extended over the area allowed for the opening, but be sure to leave the rope loop exposed. When ready for filling, a small slit is made through the paper around three edges of the area allowed for an opening. The flap can then be replaced. If you are afraid that you might forget where it is after the piñata is completed, put a small paper clip on the ruffling.

10–Fill the piñata with wrapped candies, gum, nuts, and small toys.

11–To hang, tie one end of a length of sturdy rope to the end of the harness and suspend the piñata from a tree branch or a large hook.

12–A yard, patio, or large playroom is usually a practical location for the piñata game. The players should be blindfolded, given a sturdy stick, spun around two or three times, and set free to find the piñata and attempt to break it. The piñata may be maneuvered up and down so that it evades the swinging stick of the blindfolded contestant.

For young children, the piñata may simply be tied to the top of a stool or hung low in a doorway.

SUGARPLUM BASKETS

Baskets are among the most versatile paper Christmas tree ornaments. They can be varied in many ways and are popular in many different countries. They may be made from various kinds of paper, starting with a square or a circle. All begin with paper folded and cut on alternating lines, then opened and gently pulled into shape. Small children can make baskets if someone draws light guidelines for them to cut on.

Materials

Sturdy paper (use typing paper, metallic wrapping paper,
. or construction paper)
Cellophane tape or small gummed stars

Round Basket (Basic Rule)

1–Mark a circle the size you desire. A 3- to 4-inch diameter
is good. Cut it out.
2–Fold into fourths if you want a rather open basket, into
eighths for a more delicate one.
3–Cut alternating lines as shown, marking guidelines
lightly with a pencil. Do not cut completely across the
segment but leave at least ⅛ inch.
4–Open carefully.
5–Decide if you want to hang the basket from the center or
from the edge.

To hang from the *center*, put a small piece of tape in the
center on the inside of the basket or use a gummed star on
the outside. Attach an ornament hanger made from a
partially opened paper clip, a pipe cleaner bent into a hook
shape, or make a hanging loop from yarn strung through
the reinforced center, then tied to make the loop. Gently
pull into a basket shape.

To hang from the *edge*, make the hanging loop from yarn
run under the first cut on opposite sides of the basket. Tie
to form the loop. Do not bring the basket tightly together
at the top but leave it somewhat open.

Square Basket

1–Cut a square of paper the size you desire. A 4-inch
 square is a good size to work with.
2–Fold the paper in half diagonally. Repeat on the other
 diagonal. You will have folded the square into fourths.
 If you wish a more delicate basket, fold in half on the
 diagonal again.
3–If desired, lightly mark guidelines for cutting.
4–Cut lines in alternating directions, being very careful to
 stop the cut about ⅛ inch from the edge of the fold.
5–Finish as for the round basket.

Two-Faced Baskets

Follow the Basic Rule *except:*
Before cutting the basket, glue two pieces of paper back
to back. These may be simply different colors or you may
use two pieces of metallic gift paper (do not use household
aluminum foil or decorator foil). Let the glue dry
thoroughly before you start to cut the baskets. If you have
chosen foil, fold the paper into fourths and make the cuts
slightly wider apart than with thinner paper.

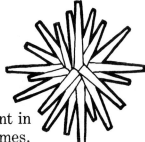

THE PORCUPINE

The porcupine is a popular Christmas tree ornament in
many countries. It sometimes goes by other names,
including a Polish star. White ones are extremely attractive, but you can make them with gold or silver paper on
the tips of the points. This is done by pasting a ¾-inch
border on the original circle before the star is made up.

Materials

White writing paper
White glue
2 tiny cardboard discs or white buttons
Sturdy white thread or cord

Method

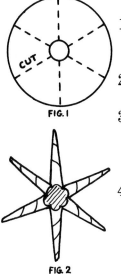

FIG. 1

FIG. 2

1–Cut ten to twelve circles, 4 inches in diameter. Fold each in half, then again in half twice more. Crease the edges to make the outline of eight sections (see figure 1).

2–Cut the circles on the creased lines, starting from the outer edge up to 1 inch of the center.

3–Using a sharpened pencil with the lead broken off, roll each section around the pencil to form a conical spike (see figure 2). Glue in place and let dry. The points should appear sharp.

4–String the completed circles together tightly, using a needle and strong thread. Use a button or tiny disc of cardboard to hold the knot of the thread, and when all the circles have been threaded, slip another over the needle. Knot the thread, leaving a 7- or 8-inch loop.

DANISH PLEATED STAR

These stars are common Christmas decorations in many areas. This is a Danish way of making them.

Materials

Gold paper, preferably double-sided, 8 inches by 20 inches
Needle

Gold or deep yellow thread
Stapler

Method

1–Fold the paper, crosswise, into one-inch pleats.
2–Keeping the pleats folded, sew through the center of all
    the pleats.
3–Cut as shown to form a star.
4–Open out the star and staple the edges together.

DANISH REED ORNAMENT

   This Danish ornament combines fine, lightweight reed,
which is available in craft shops, and gummed stars. You
may vary the dimensions as you like.

Materials

Lightweight reed
Medium-sized gummed stars
Large-sized gummed stars

Method

1–Soak the reed in water for 10 minutes to make it pliable.
2–Cut the reed into three pieces 8 inches, 9 inches, and 10
    inches long.
3–Form each piece of reed into a loop. Glue or wire the
    ends together. Let dry, then fasten all together at the
    joinings, forming a triple loop joined together at the
    top.
4–On the front and back of the smallest loop, glue three
    sets of medium-sized gummed stars back to back so

Photographed by Earl Benton
Presented by the Church of the Trinity, St. Albans, West Virginia

A living Nativity scene

Lucia crown

the ornament looks alike on both sides.

5–Do not put any stars on the middle loop.

6–On the outer loop, alternate a large, a medium, a large, a medium, and a large star. All are backed up with other stars the same size.

7–Make a hanging loop at the top of the ornament.

DANISH FRINGED BALLS

In Denmark, one often sees Christmas tree balls made from fringed double-sided gold paper. They are very handsome ornaments and easily made. If you cannot get double-sided paper, glue two sheets of single-faced gold paper together with the right sides out, or substitute decorator foil.

Materials

Double-sided gold paper, 2 inches by 8 inches
Small bead
Gold cord for hanging

Method

1–Following the diagram, cut foil as shown. Make a line about ¼ inch wide down the center of the strip. Cut fringe only to that line.
2–Use a table knife to curl the fringe as shown. Bend each section toward the center without creasing. The fringe should almost meet in the middle.
3–Roll the foil into a tight ball. Fasten with a piece of transparent tape.
4–To make the hanging loop, thread one end of cord through the bead. Knot it securely around the bead. Put the cord through the eye of the needle and run it up through the center of the ornament. Double the cord over to form your hanging loop and knot close to the top of the ball.

SWEDISH BIRD

Birds of all sorts are popular Christmas decorations. This particular one is Swedish and is traditionally suspended over the Christmas dinner table to bring good luck. Birds are also charming on the tree.

Materials

Cardboard, 6 inches square
2 strips tissue paper, 5 inches by 9 inches

Method

1–Cut the body of the bird from cardboard. Slit the body on the guidelines given, widening to about 1/16 inch so that the wings and tail can be inserted.

69

Crafts from many lands

Norwegian straw wreath

Danish baked wreath

2–Make the wings and tail by folding the tissue paper crosswise into ½-inch pleats. Staple in the middle. Notch edges of the folded strip as shown, and cut the ends into points.

3–Insert the wings and tail and secure with tiny pieces of cellophane tape.

4–Find the balance point on the back and run a hanging loop through the body, close to the edge.

DANISH WOVEN HEARTS

The nineteenth-century author Hans Christian Andersen was also skilled in paper artistry. One of his favorite shapes was the heart, and he may have been the inventor of the famous Danish woven heart. It is traditionally done in red and white, the colors of the Danish national flag. This indicates that the heart had its beginnings in the southern part of Jutland, where during wartime, the border people have frequently resorted to silent symbols in the Danish national colors to show where their hearts lay.

This method of making a Danish woven heart will produce a basket. You may add a handle and hang it on the Christmas tree. If you wish, fill it with some lightweight candy or cookies or artificial flowers. Using two colors makes the weaving simpler—as well as typically Danish!

Materials

Red and white or other colors of paper (if possible, use European construction paper)

Method

1–Use two pieces of paper three times as long as they are wide. Fold each in half lengthwise.

2—Draw a square from the fold. Lightly mark the top edge of the square. Draw a semicircle in the area above the square which will be the top of one half of the heart. Cut out on the curve.

3—To make weaving loops, draw light lines from the fold to the top of the square to mark as many strips as you will use for weaving. Cut along the lines from the fold to the top edge of the square, forming the weaving loops. The number of strips determines the size and width of the rows of weaving.

4—Place the folded halves of the heart side by side with the curved edges up. To weave, start with the top loop of the white half of the heart. Insert the white loop into the first red loop. Now open the white loop to insert the second red loop, and so on to the end of the row.

5—For the second row, turn the heart over and working with the top red loop, insert into the first loop. Continue as with the first row.

6—Repeat in this manner until the whole heart has been interwoven. Be especially careful on the bottom row; you will have very little room for moving your fingers and it is easy to tear the heart at this point.

7—Attach a strip of paper 6 inches by 1 inch to form the handle.

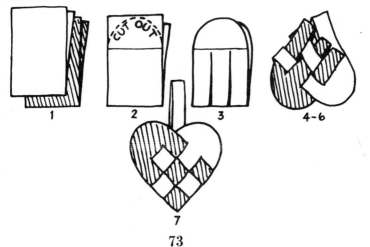

73

Piñata

Bread dough ornaments

European paper ornaments

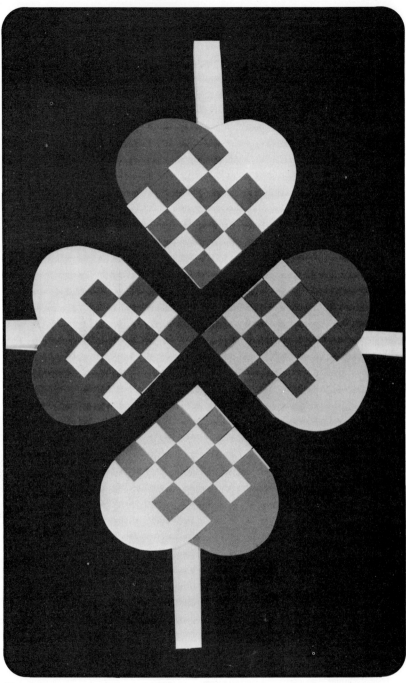

Danish woven hearts

DANISH STAR ORNAMENT

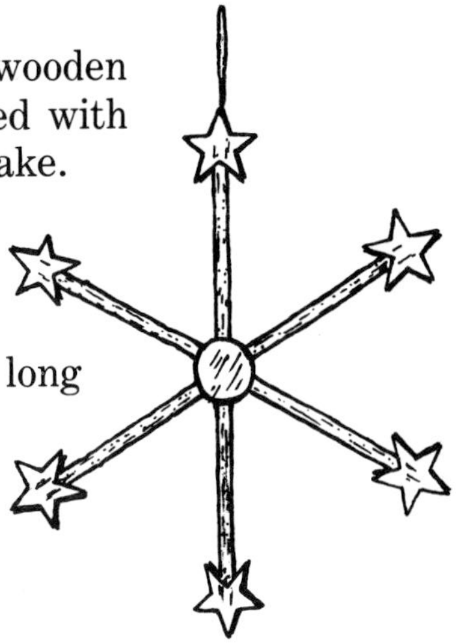

This ornament is made from toothpicks or thin wooden sticks fastened together in the center and trimmed with gummed stars. It is very attractive and easy to make.

Materials

6 wooden toothpicks or 3 thin craft sticks 6 inches long
2 gold or silver gummed circles ½ inch across
12 medium-sized gummed stars

Method

1–If using toothpicks, glue two together end to end. The round ones will have nicely butted ends. Repeat with the other toothpicks. Let dry.
2–Cross the sticks to form a six-pointed star. Glue together at the center. Let the glue set before continuing.
3–Glue two circles over the center of the ornament on either side to cover the joint.
4–Glue two stars back to back on each point of the star.
5–Make a hanging loop and attach to one of the rays of the star.

POLISH HEART ORNAMENT

Materials

Yellow paper, 6 inches square
Red paper, 6 inches square
Black paper, 6 inches square

Stained-glass cookies

Springerle

Large Heart (Basic Rule)

1–Cut two red hearts from piece 1.
2–Cut two yellow hearts from piece 2.
3–Cut two red hearts from piece 3.
4–Cut the hanging loop and glue it inside a large red heart with ½ inch of the loop inside. Glue the other red heart, right side out, on top of it.
5–Glue a yellow heart in the center of either side of the red heart.
6–Glue a small red heart in the center of either side of the yellow heart.

Middle Heart

Following the Basic Rule, cut two yellow hearts from piece 2, two black hearts from piece 3, and two red hearts from piece 4.

Small Heart

Following the Basic Rule, cut two black hearts from piece 3, two red hearts from piece 4, and two yellow hearts from piece 5.

Assemble by gluing the point of the large heart to the cleavage of the medium heart and the point of the medium heart to the cleavage of the small heart.

SCANDINAVIAN MOUSETRAPS

The mousetrap is a popular Scandinavian Christmas item. Either alone or incorporated into something else, it is interesting and different. This one is made from two contrasting colors of paper and is used as a mobile.

Materials

2 contrasting colors of paper, cut strips 1 inch wide by at least 14 inches long—or longer if you prefer
½ inch square of cardboard

Method

1–Glue two pieces of colored paper together at right angles as shown.
2–Fold the first color over the second, repeating until you have used up your paper.
3–At the top of the last fold, glue the cardboard in place. Working from the underside, through the cardboard, make your hanging loop. Knot the thread on the underside, pull it through and knot it again, cut the loop the length you want it, then tie the ends together.

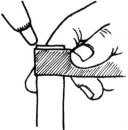

POLISH TREETOP ANGEL

There are many types of angels used on Polish Christmas trees. This one is a particular favorite; she is characteristically Polish. The angel may be used as either a tree or treetop ornament. You may decorate the angel as you like.

Materials

White cardboard, 9 inches by 12 inches
Red and blue felt-tipped pens

Polish treetop angel

The Three Wise Men

Photographed at Christ Church Episcopal, Nashville, Tennessee

Traditional crèche

Gold paper
Deep yellow paper
Scraps of colored paper, beads, sequins, fringe, etc. for
    decorating the angel

Method

1–Cut the body and wings from cardboard.
2–Cut the wing covering from yellow paper.
3–Cut the crown, skirt, bodice, and star from gold paper.
4–Cut the belt, skirt trim, and shoes from whatever you
    like. Glue cut-outs to the cardboard body.
5–Draw the angel's face with pens.
6–If you are making a treetop angel, fold a ¾-inch by 2-inch
    piece of cardboard in thirds lengthwise. Glue the
    middle section to the center back of the angel. Cut a
    piece of fairly stiff wire at least 6 inches long. Bend the
    other thirds together and pass the wire through them.
    Leave just enough wire to twist together to secure.
    Wrap the long end of the wire around the treetop.
7–To hang the angel, cut a hanging loop from fine wire.
    Pierce a small hole close to the upper center edge of
    the crown. Run the wire through and twist the ends
    together to form a loop.

84

DECORATIONS FROM THE KITCHEN

DANISH CAKE ADVENT WREATH

Materials

Pastry:
2 envelopes dry yeast or 2 cakes fresh yeast
1 cup milk, scalded
½ cup shortening
½ cup sugar
1 teaspoon salt
2 well-beaten eggs
4½ cups enriched flour

Filling:
2 tablespoons butter
¾ cup sugar
1 teaspoon cinnamon
¼ cup golden raisins
½ cup blanched, finely chopped almonds

Glaze:
1 egg yolk
2 tablespoons milk

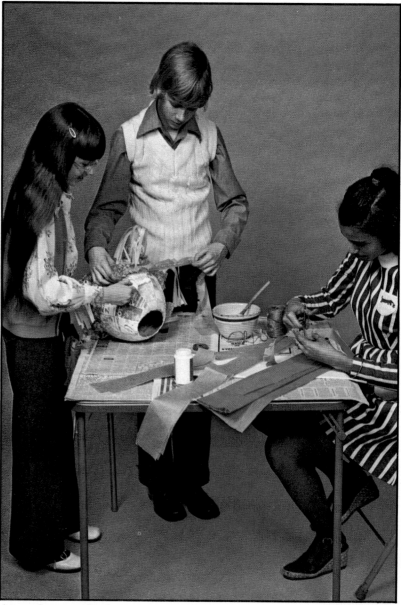

At work on a piñata

From the sewing basket

Method

1–Combine milk, shortening, sugar, and salt. Heat until shortening is melted. Cool to lukewarm. Soften the yeast in this mixture.
2–Add eggs and flour. Mix to a soft dough.
3–Knead on a lightly floured surface until smooth and elastic.
4–Place in a greased bowl, turn once, and cover with a damp cloth. Let rest in a warm place until double (about 1½ hours).
5–Punch down. Cover and let rest for 10 minutes.
6–Divide the dough into three equal parts. Roll each of these pieces into strips about 2 inches in diameter. Brush with melted butter or margarine, then roll in the sugar-nut filling. Braid the strips together, working from the middle out toward each end. Turn the ends together to form a wreath 12 inches in diameter. Place in a well-greased tube pan or on a cookie sheet.
7–Cover loosely and let rise until double (about 40 minutes).
8–Brush with the glaze and bake in a preheated 350°oven for 25 to 30 minutes.
9–Suggestions for decorating are found on page 30.

LUCIA BUNS

These delightful, saffron-flavored buns are quite easy to make. You can obtain saffron from your neighborhood grocery or specialty food shop. A few drops of yellow food coloring may be substituted. You will need to add vanilla or some other flavoring if the saffron is omitted.

Decorations from the Kitchen

Materials

Pastry:
½ cup warm water (110°-115°)
2 packages active dry yeast
1½ cups lukewarm milk
½ cup sugar
2 teaspoons salt
2 eggs
½ cup soft shortening
7 to 7½ cups sifted all-purpose flour (not self-rising)
1 teaspoon powdered saffron
Raisins for decoration

Glaze:
1 egg yolk
1 tablespoon milk

Method

1–Dissolve the saffron in two teaspoons boiling water. Strain if saffron is not powdered.
2–Warm the milk over low heat. If the milk gets too hot, cool before using to avoid killing the yeast.
3–Dissolve the yeast in warm water.
4–Add the lukewarm milk, sugar, salt, two eggs, shortening, and half of the sifted flour. Add the dissolved saffron. Stir until smooth.
5–Add the remaining flour a little at a time to make a dough which is easy to handle. You may or may not need all the flour.
6–Mix the dough with your hands. It is ready to knead when it stops sticking and pulls away from the bowl.
7–Lightly flour your work surface. Knead until the dough is smooth and elastic. This should take about five minutes or 200 turns.

Advent calendar

Gingerbread house

Lucia Buns

8–Place in a greased pan, turn once to coat the dough, cover and set in a warm (85°) place to rise. This should take about 1½ hours if the temperature is correct.

9–Punch the dough down and allow to rise again.

10–Roll out to ¼-inch thickness. Cut into strips ½-inch wide.

11–Shape according to diagrams. Do the preliminary shaping on the table, but finish putting the buns together on greased baking sheets, spacing well apart.

12–Let the buns rise on the baking sheets, covered lightly with a clean, dry towel. When they have risen, brush with a glaze made by combining the extra egg yolk with one tablespoon of milk.

13–Bake at 400° for about 10 minutes or until golden brown.

This makes from two to four dozen buns depending on the shapes used.

Lussekatter—Lucia Cats

Cut strips 5 inches to 7 inches in length. Roll as in Basic Rule. Place the rolls in pairs on the greased baking sheets, pinching the centers to join them and coiling the four ends out. Put a raisin in each coil.

Julgalt—Christmas S

Cut dough into 7-inch lengths. Roll thin strips. Shape as shown, using a raisin for each coil.

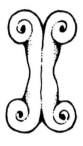

Gulluagn—Double S

Cut two strips 9 inches long for each bun. Roll. Twist each into an S and place one over the other, brushing with milk to make them stick. Put a raisin in each coil.

Decorations from the Kitchen

Praestens Har—Priest's Hair

Cut three strips of dough 7 inches long. Roll. Curl as shown, then insert one within the other. Seal with milk. Put a raisin in each coil.

Luciakrona—Crown

Cut five strips 3 inches long. Roll. Curve one strip to form the base and set the other four in place as shown. Seal with milk. Put a raisin in each coil.

Pojkar—Boys

Cut the dough into 8-inch strips. Roll. Shape as shown.

Lilja—Lily

Cut the dough into 7-inch strips. Roll. Form the lily as shown. Put raisins in each coil.

SIMPLIFIED LUCIA BUNS

If the traditional Lucia dough seems too troublesome and time-consuming, a basic sugar cookie dough may be satisfactorily used. This simplified version is adapted from Susan Purdy's book, *Christmas Decorations for You to Make*.

Materials

1 cup sweet butter or margarine
½ cup sugar

Danish woven hearts

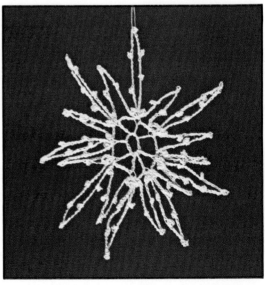

Crocheted snowflake

Scandinavian yarn doll

Luminarias

2½ cups sifted all-purpose flour

2 tablespoons vanilla extract or 1 tablespoon almond extract

Yellow food coloring

Method

1–Blend the sugar and butter and mix until fluffy.

2–Add vanilla or almond extract and several drops of yellow food coloring.

3–Add sifted flour, ½ cup at a time, mixing well. After you add all of the flour, mix with your hands.

4–Flour a pastry board. Take about ½ cup of dough at a time and roll it into narrow strips about ⅜-inch thick. Form into Lucia shapes and put on greased cookie sheets using a floured spatula. Keep them at least an inch apart so that the cookies will have room to spread.

5–Bake at 350° about 10 minutes or until golden brown. Cool. (If the dough cracks or breaks while forming into shapes pinch or pat it back together. When using dough made with real butter, warm the lumps in your hands to soften slightly before rolling out.)

6–If desired, dip raisins in a mixture of confectioner's sugar and water. Place for the features.

SPRINGERLE

For many years, Germans have painted their famous springerle—hard, anise-flavored cookies—with bright vegetable colors, producing attractive, edible ornaments. These cookies have been known in Pennsylvania Dutch country for over one hundred years and are frequently seen in Germany, especially at the Christmas markets.

It is quite easy to make these cookies. You do need a

springerle roller or board for embossing the designs. The rollers are available at holiday time in many stores and are not expensive. Most springerle are made weeks ahead, then put into a tightly closed tin with a slice of apple to age and develop the flavor. For best results, change the apple from time to time.

Materials

2 eggs
1 cup sugar
2¼ cups sifted all-purpose flour
Anise seed
Springerle roller
Vegetable colors
Clean fine-pointed artist's brushes

Method

1–Cream eggs and sugar and beat well together. The mixture should be pale yellow and very thick.
2–Add sifted flour until the dough is blended and very stiff. Refrigerate for 3 to 4 hours.
3–Roll out to a ¼-inch thickness on a lightly floured board.
4–Flour a springerle roller and press down on the dough.

5–Punch a hole close to the edge of each cookie. Cut apart. Let dry on a lightly floured board sprinkled with anise seed for at least 10 hours at room temperature.

6–Bake on a lightly greased sheet at 325° for 12 to 15 minutes. Cool.

7–Before painting, be sure there is no loose flour. Use vegetable colors and new or very clean brushes to paint the embossed designs. Let one color dry well before using a second one.

8–Cut hanging loops from bright yarn and thread through the cookies.

9–Age in tightly covered tins for at least two weeks. These cookies are often made for eating without painting them.

BERLINER KRANZE

These Norwegian Christmas wreath cookies are called Berlin Wreaths. They make a delightful addition to the Christmas tree when a piece of bright yarn is run through the center to form a hanging loop. They are also delicious.

Decorations from the Kitchen

Materials

1½ cups shortening (half butter or margarine)
1 cup granulated sugar
2 teaspoons grated orange rind
2 eggs
4 cups all-purpose flour
1 egg white
2 tablespoons sugar
Candied red cherries—at least 60, more if you prefer
Green citron

Method

1–Combine the sugar, shortening, and grated orange rind.
   Add eggs and mix well.
2–Add the sifted flour, ½ cup at a time, to the first
   mixture.
3–Cover and chill for at least one hour.
4–Cut the cherries into berry-sized bits and set aside. You
   should get at least four berries to each cherry.
5–Slice the citron about ⅛ inch thick. Cut into jagged holly
   leaves. Allow two leaves to each cookie. Since this
   recipe makes about 72 cookies, you will need approximately 144 leaves.
6–Roll small pieces of dough into pencil size—about 6
   inches long and ¼ inch thick. If the dough seems
   crumbly, work in a few drops of liquid until it sticks
   together.
7–Form each piece into a circle bringing one end over and
   through in a single knot. Leave a ½-inch end on each
   side.
8–Put the extra egg white in a small bowl and beat until
   frothy. Gradually add two tablespoons of sugar.
9–Brush each cookie with this meringue before it is baked.

Press three berries and two leaves in place on the knot of each cookie.

10–Bake at 400° on ungreased sheets until the cookies are set but not brown—about 10 to 12 minutes. Cool on racks.

11–To hang cut bright yarn into pieces twice the length you want each hanging loop to be. Slip through the center of each wreath and knot the ends tightly together.

GINGERBREAD HOUSE

Gingerbread houses have long been associated with the witch's house in Jakob Grimm's famous tale of Hansel and Gretel. Though probably of German origin, they are also a popular Christmas tradition in northern Europe and the United States.

Gingerbread houses can be used as holiday decorations

over a period of years if they are stored in a very dry place, or they can be eaten after Christmas. Making them is precision work. The pieces must be cut exactly, or they will not fit together correctly when the house is assembled.

This recipe makes one gingerbread house and at least a dozen cookies. If you roll the dough a little thinner than the recipe says, you can get two houses from it. For more information, see *Visions of Sugarplums* by Mimi Sheraton.

Materials

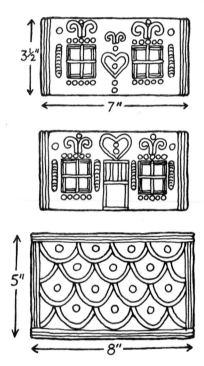

The House:
1 cup butter or margarine
1 cup firmly packed brown sugar
Grated rind of 1 lemon (optional)
2 teaspoons cinnamon
1 tablespoon ginger
1 cup golden molasses
2 eggs
6 cups all-purpose flour
½ teaspoon salt
1¼ teaspoons baking soda

The Icing:
3 egg whites
Pinch salt
4½ cups sifted confectioners' sugar
1½ teaspoons lemon juice
Pastry tube

Method

1–Following the diagrams, draw your pattern on white paper. Be extremely careful to get the measurements exact and the lines the correct distance from each other. If needed, use a protractor to get the angles correct. Extreme care should be used at this stage, since it will affect the appearance of the finished house.

2—Cream the brown sugar and butter or margarine in a large mixing bowl until it is light and fluffy. Mix in the spices and the grated lemon rind.

3—Bring the molasses to a boil over low heat. One cup dark corn syrup may be substituted for the molasses.

4—Stir the boiling molasses into the butter mixture. Blend well.

5—Add eggs and beat well.

6—Sift together 4 cups of flour, baking soda, and salt. Add these to the mixture and beat well. Use enough of the remaining flour to make the dough smooth enough to roll, but be sure it is still very soft and pliable.

7—Roll dough in waxed paper and chill for one hour.

8—After chilling the dough, divide into several sections. Place each one on a lightly floured board and roll out to ¼-inch thickness.

9—Arrange pieces of dough on two large, lightly greased baking sheets. Lay the patterns on the rolled-out dough and cut around them with a sharp knife. Cut a front and a back for the house and two of each other piece. You can use the knife to cut out windows and add doors, but keep the basic pattern the same. If you do not cut out the windows and doors, they can be drawn in with frosting.

10—Follow the pattern and you will have 10 pieces. Use the remaining dough for cookies or a second gingerbread house.

11—Bake at 350° for 15 to 20 minutes. Remove smaller pieces as they brown sooner. If the edges bake together, carefully cut them apart.

12—Let the pieces cool a few minutes on the baking sheet, then transfer them to wire racks to finish cooling.

13–While the sections cool make the decorative icing. Beat the egg whites until frothy. Add sugar, salt, and lemon juice and beat until the mixture stands in sharp peaks. Add additional sugar if necessary to make a stiff paste.

14–It is easiest to decorate the house before it is assembled. Fill a pastry tube halfway with the icing. Using a fine writing tip, draw decorations on the house pieces. Let the icing harden before assembling the house.

15–To join the sections, use a pastry tube to put a thick line of icing on one of the edges of the house, then press the adjoining edge against it. Hold in place, keeping the pieces even, until the icing sets. Let the pieces harden for a few minutes before joining the next sections. When you are finished, cover the seams with more decorative icing.

16–Set the house on a cardboard base cut a bit larger than the house. Fasten in place with decorative icing put on the bottom edges. Decorate the base in any way you like. If you want more snow on the base, make an additional batch of decorative icing.

NÜRNBURG STAR COOKIES

These big cookies are sold at the Christkindlemarkt in Nürnburg each Christmas. By adding a hanging loop, they make interesting, edible Christmas tree decorations.

Materials

Recipe for any cut-out molasses cookies, or use the recipe given for the Gingerbread House dough

Star cookie cutter or pattern—about 4½ inches across
(traditionally a six-pointed pattern is used)
Bottle lid or thimble about ¾ inch to 1 inch across

Glaze:
1 cup granulated sugar
½ cup water
¼ cup confectioners' sugar
Blanched almonds—one for each cookie point

Method

1–Roll the dough ¼-inch thick and cut with the star pattern. Place the cookies 1 inch apart on greased cookie sheets.
2–Dip the lid or thimble in flour and shake off the excess. Cut out the center of each star. Remove and bake stars as directed.
3–While the cookies are baking, make the glaze. To do this, blend the granulated sugar with water. Boil over medium heat until the first indication of a thread appears when a spoonful of syrup is dropped into cold water. If you are using a candy thermometer, it should

register 230°. Remove from the heat and stir in the confectioners' sugar.

4–As soon as the cookies come from the oven, brush with the hot glaze. Press an almond in place in the point of each star before the glaze hardens. If the glaze becomes sugary while you are brushing the cookies, reheat slightly and add a little water until it clears.

5–When the cookies are cool, make hanging loops from bright yarn. Be sure to wash off any spilled glaze before you reuse the cookie sheets.

STAINED-GLASS COOKIES

These cookies make very interesting tree ornaments as well as tasty treats. They may be made in several ways. One method uses cookie cutters or jar lids to form the outlines of the cookies, while in the other method, coils of dough are used. The inner parts are melted hard candy.

Materials

¾ cup shortening (part butter or margarine, softened)
1 cup granulated sugar
2 eggs
1 teaspoonful of vanilla extract or ½ teaspoon lemon
    extract
2½ cups all-purpose flour
1 teaspoon baking powder
1 teaspoon salt
About 6 packages of brightly colored candy mints
    or
1 pound sour balls or other, brightly colored hard candy
    or

Lollipops
    or
Candy canes (broken ones are fine)

Rolled-Out Method

1–Mix sugar, eggs, and flavoring. Blend well.
2–Sift together flour, baking powder, and salt.
3–Stir the second mixture into the first. Blend well.
4–Cover and chill for at least one hour.
5–Cover baking sheets with aluminum foil. Do not grease.
6–Roll about 1 cup of the dough on a lightly floured board to ⅛-inch thickness. Keep the remaining dough in the refrigerator.
7–Cut into desired shapes. Transfer to the baking sheets keeping them about ½ inch apart.
8–On the baking sheets, use a knife or smaller cutter to remove the center of each cookie.
9–Allow a ⅜-inch margin of dough. Carefully remove the cut-out sections. Set aside to roll out again.
10–Punch hanging holes in the cookies.
11–Put a piece of candy in the cut-out section of each cookie. If you use crushed candy, fill the space evenly without piling it. If the cut-out has points—like a star—be sure that there is candy in the points. Try not to spill candy on the dough. It will melt during the baking and spoil the design.
12–Bake at 375° for 7 to 9 minutes or until lightly browned and the candy has melted. Use a metal spatula to spread any unmelted candy. Repunch the holes while the cookies are hot.
13–Allow the cookies to cool completely before removing them from the baking sheets. If necessary, carefully slip off the foil with the cookies still on it.
14–To hang, cut loops from brightly colored yarn and string it through the punched out holes.

Coil Method

If you do not have cookie cutters or prefer to be more creative, make your cookies this way. Be sure that the outline pieces are joined for strength.

1–Roll dough into long thin strips about ¼-inch thick.
2–Form into outlines of the shapes that you want. Do this directly on the baking sheet. If you want designs in the centers of the cookies, make them with narrower strips of dough. These center strips do not have to connect with the rest of the cookie.
3–Fill with candy.
4–Punch hanging holes in the cookies.
5–Bake and cool as for the cut-out cookies, but bake these at least 10 minutes. Insert the hanging loops.

BREAD DOUGH ORNAMENTS

In a number of European countries and in parts of South America, edible ornaments made of bread dough are popular Christmas docorations.

The Finnish bread dough doll faces are perhaps the best known. They are called *Pullaukkoja* and are decorated only with raisins or currants to mark their features.

In Switzerland, the figures are called *Grittibanz*, and they vary in size from 8 to 24 inches. The girl cookies have their hair done in braids and wear skirts made from the dough. Boys are dressed in bread-dough shorts and wear Alpine hats. Their features are marked with raisins.

In Germany, figures of St. Nicholas or Krampus are often made from bread dough. They are usually at least a foot tall and carry a real twig from a cherry branch. There are also elaborate reindeer made from bread dough. All are highly glazed with a mixture of egg yolk and milk.

Decorations from the Kitchen

To make these figures, use the recipe given for Lucia buns or any good dough for white bread.

In South America, the making of bread dough figures has developed into an elaborate folk art. Originally used as an offering on All Souls Day, November 2, the figures gradually came to be used as Christmas tree ornaments. In Ecuador and Guatemala, the carefully modeled dolls are decorated with brilliantly colored sugar icing. In Peru, bright feather headdresses are often added.

These dough figures can be made from baker's clay. The dough ornaments last only one year, but those made from clay can be reused again and again.

Each material has its advantages and disadvantages. Since the bread dough rises in the baking, detailing is limited. Also, because these ornaments are edible, the only possible coloring for them is food coloring. Though the baker's clay ornaments are inedible and may be colored with all kinds of materials, they cannot be made very large. If they are, the clay will not harden throughout, and the figures may crack and fall apart. The following is a recipe for baker's clay.

Materials

1 cup uniodized salt
3 to 4 cups unsifted flour
1¼ to 1½ cups water

Method

1–Combine the ingredients, working until pliable. Knead as for regular bread, adding more water if needed.

2–The dough sculpture may be formed directly on a well-greased cookie tin or on a board from which it can be transferred. Keep hands well-floured. To build up where depth or layer effect is required, coat the bottom layer with water before adding to it. Delicate sections—extensions and thin pieces—can be reinforced with lengths of toothpicks embedded in the dough. If the sculpture is to be hung, be sure to leave a hole for later insertion of the twine.

3–Place on a high rack in a slow oven. Bake for 2 to 4 hours, depending on the shade of darkness desired. The resulting bread is very hard. If a piece breaks off, repair it with household white glue.

4–Paint after the sculpture is cool. Don't expect the dough to come out even in color; it won't.

PLAY CLAY ORNAMENTS

Play clay is a familiar substance wherever there are small children. It is easily made, contains nothing harmful, and is very versatile. It lasts a month or more if stored in a tightly covered plastic bag in the refrigerator. Play clay dries very hard, though it will break if dropped, and may be successfully painted. If tempera paints are used, spray the finished ornament with a colorless acrylic spray to make the decorations waterproof. Uncolored clay may be used to make somewhat more complicated ornaments. Clay may be tinted by kneading food coloring into the dough before the ornaments are formed. Wet play clay ornaments will dry faster if they are placed to dry in a warm place. A screen suspended between two chairs is an ideal place to dry them. This is more than a one day project.

Materials

2 cups baking soda
1 cup cornstarch
1¼ cups water
Simple metal cookie cutters, preferably ones with both
  ends open
Plastic drinking straw
Tempera paints or acrylics
Brushes
Acrylic spray

Method

1–To make the play clay, combine the baking soda and
  cornstarch. Mix well. Add about ½ cup water, mix,
  then stir in the rest of the water. Bring to a boil over
  medium heat, stirring constantly. When it reaches the
  consistency of moist mashed potatoes, remove from
  the heat and turn onto a plate. Cover with a damp
  cloth until cool.
2–Knead the cooled mixture for a few minutes. Place in a
  plastic bag and store until you are ready to use the
  clay.
3–Sprinkle your working surface lightly with cornstarch.
  Roll out the clay to a ¼-inch thickness.
4–Cut out shapes with the cookie cutters.
5–Before the shapes harden, punch a hanging hole with the

111

cop. 3

straw. Blow on the opposite end of the straw to clear out the clay.

6–Transfer the ornaments to a drying surface with a spatula. They must dry flat. If possible, put them on an old window screen to dry so that air circulates under them as well as over them.

7–Allow to dry until the clay is completely hard. The exact time will depend on the humidity and temperature of the room as well as the thickness of the ornaments.

8–Paint the dry ornaments as you like. If you want to use more than one color of tempera, spray with a light coating of acrylic spray. Let it dry for a few seconds, then apply color as desired with tempera paints. Spray the finished ornament with acrylic.

9–If you want to use glitter on these ornaments, brush with a thin coating of glue on the area where you want the glitter. Sprinkle and shake off the excess. Let dry.

10–Cut the hanging cord twice the length you want it. String through the hole and tie to form the loop.

Variation

Play clay ornaments can be more creative to appeal to older children. The clay for this variation should be of a softer consistency than for the rolled ornaments. If you find that the clay is too firm, mix in a little more water and knead again. Be careful not to get the clay too wet.

1–Draw a freehand design and transfer to a ½-inch graph paper. Do not attempt to make these ornaments very large or they will be too heavy.

2–Slide each pattern under waxed paper on a working surface where the ornaments can be left undisturbed until they are firm enough to move.

3–Fill a pastry tube with the clay and use a medium writing

point. Squeeze, making tight squiggles rather than a straight line, onto the waxed paper over the patterns.

4—Allow the ornaments to dry. Peel off the waxed paper backing.

5—If there is any wetness remaining on the underside of the ornaments, hang until completely dry. Hang as in the Basic Rule.

ICE-CREAM CONE HORNS OF PLENTY

Except for the nylon net covering, this horn of plenty is completely edible. They resemble the cornucopias often seen on English Christmas trees.

Materials

1 pointed ice-cream cone for each horn
Assortment of small, lightweight candies
Nylon net in bright colors
Rubber band
Gift wrap ribbon
Tiny artificial flowers, if desired

113

Method

1–Cut the net in squares large enough to cover the cone completely and to form a ruffle around the top when gathered. Allow one for each horn.
2–Fill the cone with candies.
3–Stand the cone, pointed end down, in the center of the square. Bring the net up around the cone, gathering the edges into a ruffle at the top.
4–Secure with the rubber band.
5–Cut the ribbon into lengths about 2 feet long.
6–Fold in half. About 3 inches from the folded end, make a knot to form a hanging loop. Tie the rest of the ribbon tightly around the rubber band. Finish with a bow.
7–If desired, place tiny artificial flowers under the ribbon.

HOW TO HANG FRUIT ON
THE CHRISTMAS TREE

Apples were one of the very first Christmas tree ornaments, and they have traditionally been associated

114

with the Tree of Paradise and signified man's expulsion from the Garden of Eden. Decorating with apples and with oranges and lemons makes a truly old-fashioned Christmas tree. Because of the weight of the fruit, they are best used on trees with sturdy branches.

Materials

Fruit
Colored string
Nylon net

Method

1–Select fruit for its color and shape. Wash thoroughly and polish with a soft cloth.
2–For the apples, measure off lengths of colored string to make tying loops. Double the string and knot the ends tightly around the stem of each apple.
3–The lemons and oranges can be hung by placing them in a square of nylon net two inches larger than the fruit. Gather at the top and tie a loop to hang.

HOW TO HANG CANDY AND DROP COOKIES ON THE CHRISTMAS TREE

Fairly small, lightweight drop cookies or candy may be used on the Christmas tree. Cut squares of bright colored cellophane or tissue wrap at least two inches larger than the cookies. Place the cookie in the center of the square and gather the edges up around the cookie. Cut a piece of string about twice as long as you want the hanging loop to be. Tie one end of the string tightly around the gathered edge of the cellophane or plastic wrap. Double the end over to form a loop. Knot together.

To hang lollipops, cut a piece of brightly colored string into lengths twice as long as you want the hanging loops to be. Tie the ends together and fasten to the lollipop stick with gummed tape.

DECORATIONS FROM THE SEWING BASKET

SCANDINAVIAN YARN DOLLS

Yarn dolls are popular Christmas tree decorations in Scandinavia, especially in Norway and Sweden. There are several ways of making them. Scraps of yarn left over from knitting or crocheting projects are useful for making the dolls. Bright colors, particularly red, are best for these dolls.

Materials

About 8 yards medium- to heavyweight yarn
Embroidery cotton

Cardboard-Wrapped Method (Basic Rule)

1–Cut one piece of cardboard 6 inches long by 4 inches wide.
2–Cut another piece of cardboard 4 inches long by 2 inches wide.
3–Depending on the weight of the yarn, wrap it thirty to

117

forty times around the length of the 6-inch cardboard. Cut the end.

4–Slip a 3-inch piece of yarn under one end of the wrapped section. Pull tightly and tie the ends together in a firm knot. Slip the yarn off the cardboard. This will be the top of the doll's head.

5–About an inch below the top of the head, tie tightly again to complete the doll's head.

6–To make arms, wind yarn about fifteen times around the length of the 4-inch cardboard. Cut the end. Slip off the cardboard.

7–With short lengths of yarn, tie tightly close to each end to form the hands.

8–Insert the arms between the yarn under the doll's head. Position.

9–Tie tightly again, below the arms. For a neater doll, have all knots at the back of the figure.

10–For a boy doll, divide the yarn below the waist in half lengthwise. Tie each section ½ inch from the bottom to complete the legs. For a girl doll, clip the yarn loops at the bottom to form her skirt.

11–Embroider the face, using colored yarn or embroidery cotton. If desired, dress the dolls.

12–Insert a hanging loop under the tie at the top of the head. Knot the ends.

Folded Method

Some people find this variation easier to do than the wrapped method. It is slightly larger than the other doll.

1–Cut thirty to forty 18-inch lengths of yarn, depending on the weight of the yarn.

2–Group these pieces together lengthwise and tie together at the center. Fold the tied yarn in half.

4—Tie tightly again 1½ inches from the first tying. This forms the doll's head.

5—Separate enough strands on each side to form arms. Tie tightly at the wrist and cut off excess yarn.

6—Tie the doll's body loosely at the waist.

7—For a boy doll, divide the remaining strands of yarn into two equal parts to form the legs, and tie each leg tightly at the ankles.

8—For a girl doll, leave as is. Trim to even the edges, if necessary.

9—To make a face, use colored yarn to tie knots around two or three threads where you want the features to be. Hang as in Basic Rule.

TOMTE

A Tomte is a Swedish elf who lives in dark corners or under boards. At Christmas, the Tomtar hide surprise packages in strange places for children.

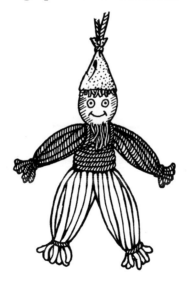

Christmas Crafts For Everyone

Materials

2 yards red yarn
2 yards gray yarn
½-inch wooden bead
2- and 4-inch squares of cardboard
Pipecleaner
Twine
Scraps of red cloth or felt
Felt-tipped pens

Method

1–To form the head, glue one end of a pipe cleaner inside the ½-inch wooden bead.
2–When dry, draw a face with felt-tipped pens.
3–Cut a ¼-inch piece of twine and ravel it out. Glue on the Tomte's forehead to form bangs.
4–Measure the circumference of the bead above the face. Cut a scrap of red cloth or felt so that it is 1½ inches wide and about ¼ inch longer than the measurement around the forehead. Glue the short ends together, forming a ¼-inch overlap. Let dry and carefully glue to the Tomte's head.
5–Gather the top edge of the hat. Tie tightly with a 7-inch piece of red yarn. Knot the ends of the yarn to make a hanging loop. Set aside.
6–Make the body with 2 yards of gray yarn, winding it six times around a 4-inch length of cardboard. Cut and knot the ends. Slip the yarn off the cardboard.
7–Using red yarn, tie tightly about ½ inch from each end.
8–Fold the yarn diagonally in half.
9–Trim the pipe cleaner glued to the head so that the end is about ½ inch long. Dip into white glue.
10–Separate the strands of yarn at the fold and insert the pipe cleaner. Press so that the yarn sticks to the neck. Set aside to dry while you make the arms.

11–Wind 1 yard of red yarn six times around a 2-inch piece of cardboard. Slip off and tie tightly with red yarn about ¼ inch from each end.

12–Slip the arms into place as in the Basic Rule.

13–Tie loosely just below the arms using red yarn.

14–Cut a piece of twine about 1 inch long. Ravel it out. Glue to the Tomte's chin to form a beard.

MOLDED STRING CAGES

These ornaments are fun to make but are very, very messy. Cover your work area with several layers of newspapers or a plastic drop cloth before you start to work. Wear old clothes or an apron and have something handy for wiping your hands as you go along.

Materials

Mercerized crochet cotton (each string cage will take about 30 yards if it is the size of a grapefruit)

A round balloon for each ornament (they are easier to make if you choose a color which contrasts with your string)

Glitter or tiny gummed stars, if desired

1 tablespoon laundry starch

2 tablespoons cold water

1 cup boiling water

Method

1–To prepare the glue, dissolve the starch in cold water. Add boiling water, stirring constantly. Cook over medium heat, stirring often, for three minutes. Allow to cool enough to handle easily. This mixture should be used the day it is made.

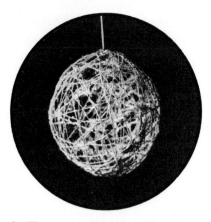

2–Blow up the balloon until it is the size of an orange or grapefruit. Tightly knot the top to keep the air in.

3–Knot one end of the crochet thread around the top of the balloon, leaving about a 3-inch end. Do not break off.

4–Carefully dip about 2 yards of the thread in the glue. Wipe off the excess, taking care not to knot.

5–Wind the soaked thread around the balloon, working from top to bottom, around the middle and around on a diagonal. Work as your imagination takes you, but do not leave any space larger than the end of your finger. You will have to get inside to remove the balloon, so do not wind the string too closely, either.

If you like, wind part of the ornament with one color thread and part with a different, contrasting thread. Tuck the end of the second color under the first and keep winding.

6–As you finish with one soaked section of thread, soak the next. Sprinkle with glitter if desired. Clip string.

7–Hang the balloon up to dry. The drying time will depend on the temperature and the humidity. Allow at least 24 hours.

8–When the string is completely dry, even at the bottom, puncture the balloon and carefully pull it out. You may need to cut away the top section.

9–Make a hanging loop from extra thread or use a regular ornament hanger.

CROCHETED SNOWFLAKES

Anyone who likes to crochet and does not have much storage room might enjoy trimming a whole tree in nothing but these snowflakes. They are charming done in white or silver and take little room between seasons.

Materials

J.&P. Coats Metallic Knit-Cro-Sheen—1 ball silver or white (1 ball makes 2 ornaments)
Steel crochet hook #1
Spray starch

Abbreviations

ch .... chain
sc .... single crochet
dc .... double crochet
sl st ..... slip stitch
sp .... space
rnd ...... round
beg ...... beginning
(*Repeat whatever follows the * as many times as specified.)

Four-Inch Tasseled Snowflake

Use 2 strands held together throughout.
Starting at the center with 2 strands of cotton held together, ch 5. Join with a sl st to form a ring. 1st round: ch 3, 11 dc in the ring. Join with a sl st to the top of chain 3.
2nd round: ch 3, dc in the same stitch as the joining, ch 6. * skip 2 dc, 2 dc in the next dc, ch 6. Repeat from * twice

123

more. Join to the top of ch 3-4 ch-6 loops.

3rd round: ch 3, dc in the same st as the joining, ch 3, 2 dc in the next dc, ch 7, * 2 dc in the next dc, ch 3, 2 dc in the next dc, ch 7. Repeat from * twice more. Join.

4th round: slip stitch in the next dc and in the next ch-3 sp, ch 3, in the same sp make 2 dc, ch 3 and 3 dc, ch 9, * skip ch-7 loop, in the next ch-3 sp make 3 dc, ch 3, 3 dc and ch 9. Repeat from * around. Join.

5th round: ch 3, dc in the next 2 dc, in the next ch-3 sp make 2 dc, ch 3 and 2 dc, dc in the next 3 dc, ch 9 * dc in the next 3 dc, in the next sp make 2 dc, ch 3 and 2 dc, dc in the next 3 dc, ch 9. Repeat from * around. Join.

6th rnd: ch 3, sl st in 3rd ch from hook—picot made; make 2 more picots, skip next 3 dc, sc in the next dc, make 3 picots, sc in the next dc, make 3 picots, skip 3 dc, sl st in the next dc, 9 sc in the next ch-9 loop, sl st in the next dc. Repeat from * around, ending with sl st in joining. Break off and fasten.

Hanger: Cut a 13-inch double strand of thread and fold in half to form a loop. Draw looped end through center picot in any corner, draw ends through loop and pull up tightly. Tie ends together.

Tassel: Wind double strand of yarn 20 times around a 4-inch piece of cardboard. With a separate double strand, tie at one end, cut at opposite end. Wind and tie another strand around tassel ½-inch from tied end. Trim evenly. Attach tassel to center picot at opposite corner from hanger. Pin snowflake to measurement on a padded surface with the wrong side up. Starch with spray starch. Dry.

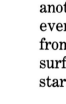

Six-Inch Snowflake

Use 2 strands held together throughout.
Starting at the center, ch 5. Join with sl st to form a ring.

Decorations from the Sewing Basket

1st rnd: ch 3, 11 dc in ring. Join with sl st to top of ch 3.

2nd rnd: Ch 8, skip next dc * dc in next dc, ch 5, skip next dc. Repeat from * around. Join last ch 5 to 3rd ch of ch-8.

3rd rnd: ch 1, sc in same st as joining, ch 4, skip 2 ch sts, dc in next ch, ch 4 * sc in next dc, ch 4, skip next 2 ch sts, dc in next ch, ch 4. Repeat from * around. Join with sl st to first sc.

4th rnd: ch 1, sc in same st as joining, ch 6, dc in next dc, ch 6. * sc in next sc, ch 6, dc in next dc, ch 6. Repeat from * around. Join to first sc.

5th rnd: sl st in each of the next 6 ch sts and in next dc, ch 16 * skip next sc, dc in next dc, ch 13. Repeat from * around. Join to 3rd ch of ch-16.

6th rnd: ch 14, * in the next dc make (dc, ch 3) twice and dc—corner made; ch 11. Repeat from * around ending with (dc in joining, ch 3) twice. Join to 3rd ch of ch 14.

7th rnd: ch 1, sc in same st as joining * ch 3, sl st in 3rd ch from hook—picot made; skip next ch, sc in next ch, (make picot, skip next ch, sc in next ch,) 4 times, picot, skip next ch (sc in next dc, picot, skip next ch, sc in next ch, picot, sc in next dc) twice. Repeat from * around, ending last repeat with picot. Join to first sc. Break off and fasten.

Hanger: Cut a 13-inch double strand of thread and fold in half to form a loop. Draw looped end through picot at tip of any point, draw ends through loop and pull up tightly. Tie ends together. Pin snowflake to measurement on a padded surface with wrong side up. Starch with spray starch. Allow to dry.

PAPER DECORATIONS
FROM MANY LANDS

PAPER STARS

Stars have had an important place in Christmas decorations everywhere. If we know an easy way to construct stars of various types, it can make decorating the Christmas tree quite simple.

The five-pointed star is widely known as the Epiphany Star and represents the star that shone over the stable where the Christ Child lay, leading the Wise Men to Bethlehem. The Epiphany Star usually accompanies Nativity scenes and is the most widely used of the different types of stars. The opinions about the use of this star vary. In some places the Epiphany Star is not used until January 6. Some authorities feel that the only suitable star for use before that time is the six-pointed Creator's Star, often called the Star of David.

Five-Pointed Star—Rectangular Folded Method

1–Use a piece of paper 8½ inches by 11 inches to make a 6-inch star. You can vary the size paper in any way you like to get smaller or larger stars. Just be sure to keep the proportions the same. Fold the paper in half

126

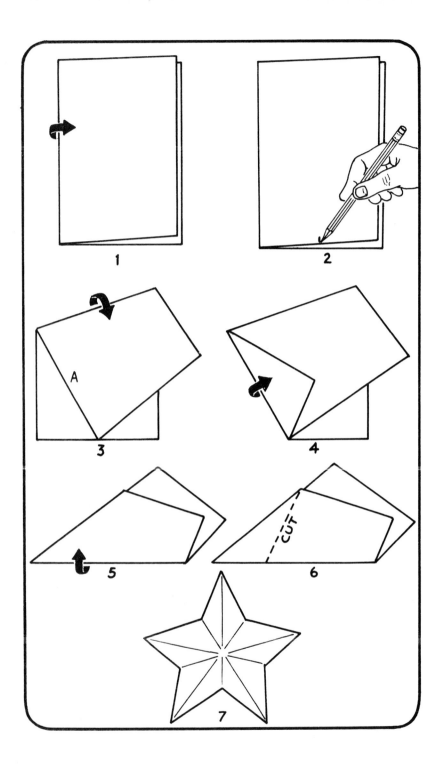

1

2

3

A

4

5

6

CUT

7

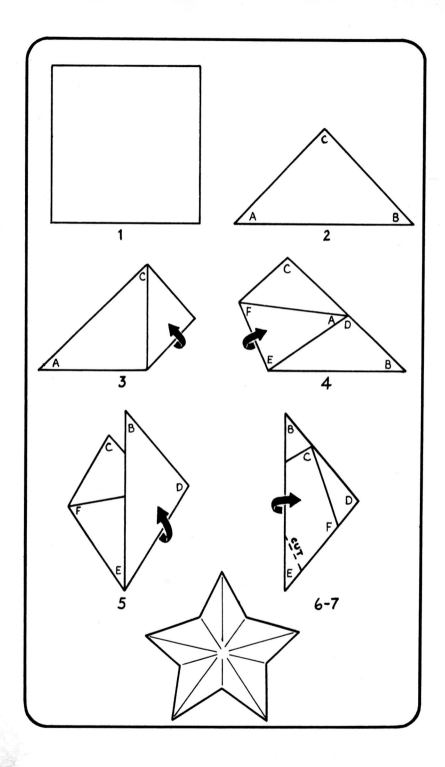

1

2

3

4

5

6-7

with the short sides together and the fold on the left-hand side.

2–Make a mark at the center of the lower edge of the folded sheet.

3–Bring the upper left-hand corner of the paper down to the mark. Crease the fold. Mark the center of the left-hand edge A as shown.

4–Fold the lower left-hand corner over the top sheet, making the fold meet A.

5–Fold the lower left-hand edge over the upper right-hand side (this will fold the paper in half).

6–Cut sharply on the diagonal across the fold.

7–Open the finished star.

Five-Pointed Star—Square Folded Method

1–Use a square of paper any size you like.

2–Fold the square diagonally in half. Have the fold at the bottom. Mark lightly in pencil the left-hand corner A, the top point C, and the right-hand corner B.

3–Fold B to C. Unfold. Lightly mark the top edge of the fold D.

4–Fold A to D. Mark the upper left-hand corner F and the lower corner E.

5–Lift point B and fold over.

6–Lift FC and fold over. You are actually folding the shape in half. Be sure that the inner edge of EC evenly meets BC so that the star will be even.

7–Cut as shown to get the star.

Six-Pointed Star

Compared to the five-pointed version, six-pointed stars are very simple to make. They can be cut into snowflakes by snipping pieces from the edges before unfolding.

1–Fold a square of paper in half on the diagonal.
2–Fold it in half on the diagonal again.
3–Fold this form in thirds as shown.
4–Cut on a sharp diagonal to form the points of the star.

CORKSCREWS OR CURLS

These simple ornaments are popular with children in many parts of the world. They may be made in a variety of sizes and from different materials. Though corkscrews are usually made from circles, they may be effectively made from squares or diamonds following the same basic directions.

Materials

Any stiff paper or decorator foil (do not attempt to use kitchen foil; it is too light to work well)

Method

1–Draw a pattern on the paper as shown.
2–Start at the outer edge and cut in a continuous line working in towards the center. Make the coil at least ¼ inch wide—wider if you are making one from a large shape. Leave a solid bit at least ¼ inch wide in the middle.
3–Fasten an ornament hanger made from a paper clip, piece of string, or a bent pipe cleaner to the solid bit in the center.

PATTERN

130

PAPER CHAINS

Paper chains are one of the oldest types of Christmas tree decorations. They can be made from any kind of paper stiff enough to hold its shape though usually construction paper is used. To make a simple chain, cut the paper into strips the width you want your links to be. Glue ends of strip together to form a link, interlocking each new link as it is glued with the preceding one. Chains are popular in many countries. They are very effective made in white paper and set off against the dark green branches of the Christmas tree.

Materials

Construction paper

Polish Chain (Basic Rule)

1–Trace a pattern for the double circle.
2–Fold the paper in half lengthwise.
3–Place the edge of the pattern on the fold and cut out.
4–Cut out the center of each circle. Make as many double circles as you will need.
5–Leave the first circle folded in half. Open the second and fold it loosely in half lengthwise.
6–Slip through the opening in the first circle. Fold the second circle in half again, and smooth out.
7–Repeat until the chain is as long as you want it to be.

PATTERN

Keyhole Chain

1–Trace the pattern.
2–Fold strips of paper, 3¼ inches by 7¼ inches, in half lengthwise, then in half crosswise.

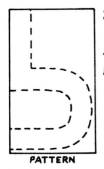

PATTERN

3–Place the stem of the keyhole against the lengthwise fold. Have the short end at the crosswise fold.

4–Cut as many keyholes as you need.

5–To make chain, link one keyhole through another. Repeat until chain is desired length.

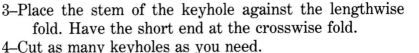

Triangle Chain

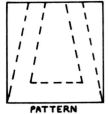

PATTERN

1–Trace the pattern.

2–Fold strips of paper, 2¼ inches by 4¼ inches, in half crosswise.

3–Place the open end of the triangle on the fold.

4–Cut out as many triangles as you need. Construct chain as in Basic Rule.

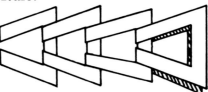

Polish Stars and Straws Chain

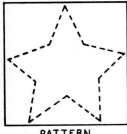

PATTERN

1–Cut out stars using the pattern illustrated on page 127 or 128 in as many colors as possible. You will need a great many stars.

2–Cut thin paper drinking straws into 1½-inch lengths, cutting the ends slightly on the diagonal. You will need twelve lengths of straws for each star so plan on cutting a large quantity.

3–Thread the needle with crochet cotton but do not break it off.

4–To make the chain, follow a star with twelve segments of straws, putting the needle through the center of each one on a slight diagonal. Add another star. Repeat until the chain is as long as you want it. This chain is a bit bulky but it is very lightweight.

Variations

1–Cut a simple paper chain from the pages of the comic section in the newspaper, from a department store catalog, or from wallpaper samples.
2–Make chain links from self-stick ribbon. Moisten one end slightly and join. Repeat for the entire chain.
3–Use pinking shears (not good ones!) to cut the links.

TISSUE PAPER GARLANDS

Tissue paper garlands are popular in many countries, though they are seen most often on Yugoslavian or Polish trees. They are simple to make but must be handled carefully since the fragile paper tends to tear easily.

Materials

Tissue paper—preferably white, but any color may be used

Method

1–Cut the paper into 3-inch widths any length you like.
2–Fold vertically into thirds.
3–Alternate slits as shown, cutting about ⅛ inch to ¼ inch from the edge.
4–Open the paper very carefully.
5–If a longer garland is desired, join shorter lengths together with rubber cement.

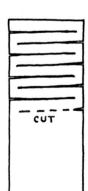

CUT

Variations

1–Use metallic wrapping paper instead of tissue paper. For young children, consider making the garland from lightweight construction paper.
2–Use pinking shears instead of regular scissors.
3–Cut in different widths for wider or narrower garlands.
4–Cut the slits on the diagonal instead of vertically.
5–Fold the paper into fourths or fifths instead of thirds.

FRINGE FESTOONING

Fringe festooning is a type of garland but much more fragile and harder to handle. It is attractive on delicate Christmas trees such as cedars. Like garlands, the strips may be joined together with rubber cement to make longer lengths. A piece of paper 6 inches by 8 inches pleated in ⅝-inch pleats will yield a 12-foot length of festooning. The highly fragile nature of this type of garlanding makes it unsuitable for use with young children or anyone who lacks good finger control.

Materials

White or colored paper (do not attempt to use paper any heavier than tissue or typing paper)

Method

1–The size paper used should not be much larger than 9 inches by 12 inches. Fold the paper into accordion pleats, working either vertically or horizontally. Be sure that the pleats are not too thick to cut easily and keep them even. Pleats ½-inch to ¾-inch wide work well with most paper.

2–Cut alternate slits as in the garland.

3–Carefully open the sheet and flatten it.

4–Cut crosswise on the folds, alternating the directions of the rows and being sure to stop cutting about ⅛ inch or slightly more from the edge. You will have one long, continuous strip. Make absolutely certain that you cut on the fold lines; if you do not, the festooning will fall apart.

PAPER MOON

A favorite Polish folk character is Pan Twardowski, who was condemned to spend the rest of time sitting in the moon as punishment for a serious misdeed. Perhaps this moon face is supposed to represent Mr. Twardowski. (If possible, use glazed paper for this ornament and fold it in half before you cut the pieces.)

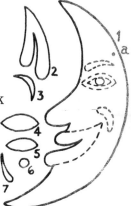

Materials

Construction paper (red, yellow, white, bright blue, dark blue, and black)
Household white glue

Method

1–Cut out piece 1 from yellow paper; piece 2 from red; piece 3 from white; piece 4 from bright blue; piece 5

135

from dark blue; and pieces 6 and 7 from black. Transfer the markings to the outside of piece 1. You will need two pieces from each pattern.

2–Glue the wrong sides of the two moons together.

3–Following the pattern, glue the features in place on both sides of the moon.

4–Thread a needle with string for the hanging loop. Insert at "a" and tie the ends together in a knot.

POLISH MUSHROOM—MUCHOMOREK OR GRZYB

Red-topped mushrooms are very popular Christmas tree decorations in Europe. They are seen in the Christmas markets in Germany and are common in Poland.

Materials

6-inch square of bright red Contac paper or construction paper (Contac paper will give you a more authentic-looking mushroom because it is brighter and more like European construction paper)
White construction paper
Cotton balls or medical cotton
Small bead
Paper punch

Method

1–Cut the top of the mushroom from red paper. If you use Contac paper, strip the backing and stick onto a sheet of white paper. Cut the top of the mushroom from this double piece. Glue the top of the mushroom together to form a cone.

2–Use the paper punch to cut out twenty white dots from white paper. Glue to the top of the mushroom.

3–Cut a piece of red or white string twice the length you want the hanging loop to be. Knot the end. String the bead on the hanging loop.

4–From the inside point of the mushroom top, push the threaded needle through, pulling the bead tight up against the point. Knot the thread close to the top of the mushroom on the outside, cut, and knot the ends.

5–Cut the stem of the mushroom from white paper and glue it together to form a cylinder. Fill with cotton and allow a little to protrude from the bottom. With a piece of red or white thread, tie the tube lightly close to the bottom. Glue in place inside the top of the mushroom.

SEGMENTED PAPER ORNAMENTS

Segmented paper ornaments seem to be universally popular. They can be made from almost any shape, folded in half, then piled up in multiples of at least three. The shapes are stapled or glued exactly on the fold so that the ornament is many-sided. You may use any double-faced kind of paper you like. Construction paper is commonly used and tissue paper is effective if enough sheets are used. Make a hanging loop by gluing a loop of string to the top of the ornament.

Materials

Construction paper in several colors
Household white glue or tape, if desired
Tracing paper
Stapler

Swedish Pig (Basic Rule)

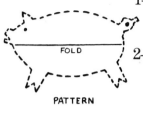

1–Using the pattern, cut four pink pigs the desired size from construction paper, marking the fold line on all four.

2–Cut the hanging loop twice the length you want it, adding 1 inch. Double the loop and tape or glue to the back of one of the segments. Have the ends about ½ inch inside the pig.

3–Fold the pigs along the line marked and staple once in the middle carefully lining up the edges. Unfold the sections to complete the pig.

Austrian Double Stars

Children in Austria often make ornaments like these. Other simple shapes such as Christmas trees, bells, hearts, and snowmen can be used as well.

1–Cut out two figures of the same shape for each ornament.

2–Slit as shown.

3–Join the two parts at the slit then open out.

4–Make a hanging loop from matching or contrasting string and tape or staple in place.

Segmented Christmas Ball

1–Cut out nine circles 3 to 4 inches in diameter from red or green paper.

2–Fold each in half and crease through the center. Open the circles up and stack together.

3–Staple the circles together along the crease at the top, bottom, and in the middle.

4–Use a small amount of glue to fasten the outer edges of a

pair of segments about a fourth of the way down. Repeat about a fourth of the way up with the next pair. Alternate top and bottom all around the circle. Press gently until the glue dries.

5–To hang, thread a needle and run through the center top of all nine circles.

ŚWIAT—THE WORLD

This ornament is called the world, *świat* in Polish, because of its spherical shape. At one time it was made from the Oplatek, the Christmas wafer, but because of the difficulty in handling and obtaining the fragile Oplatek, it is now made of construction paper or foil-covered cardboard. The size is determined by the circles.

In Polish homes, the świat is one of the central and most important ornaments on the Christmas tree. When made of the Oplatek, it demanded certain respect. After the tree was taken down, the świat was carefully hung from the ceiling. Delicate, light, and suspended by a thread, it moved in the warm air and gave beauty and enjoyment to the household until the next year.

Because of the nature of this ornament, it should not be attempted by anyone with less than good finger control. The cuts must be accurately made and assembly is tricky for anyone.

Materials

Colored construction paper or thin foil-covered cardboard
Compass

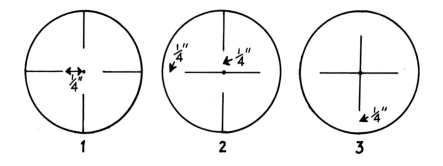

1	2	3

Method

1–Using the compass, draw three equal circles. Cut them out.

2–Using a straight edge, mark lines on the circles as shown.

3–Cut along each marked line. The exact length of the lines will depend on the diameter of the circles, but be sure to leave ¼ inch between the cut and the center of the circle, or the edge as indicated.

4–Fold circle 1 lightly in half and insert through the center of circle 2 and flatten out to form a single circle.

5–Fold 1 and 2 lightly in half along center cut of circle 2 and insert through the center of circle 3. Open and interlock into a ball by gently opening circle 2 and easing circle 1 into place.

6–Make a hanging loop.

Variation

Make the same type of ornament by using squares or diamonds cut in the same way as you cut the circles to make the świat. Follow the diagram for the placing of the cuts.

BIBLIOGRAPHY

Better Homes and Gardens. *Holiday Decorations You Can Make*. Des Moines: Meredith Publishing Company, 1974.

Brock, Virginia. *Piñatas*. Nashville: Abingdon, 1966.

Chrisman, Irma. *Christmas Trees, Decorations and Ornaments*. Great Neck, N.Y.: Hearthside Press, 1956.

Coffey, Ernestine, and Minton, Dorothy. *Designs for a Family Christmas*. Great Neck, N.Y.: Hearthside Press, 1964.

Hazelton, Nika. *The Cooking of Germany*. New York: Time-Life Books, 1969.

Ickis, Marguerite. *Folk Arts and Crafts*. New York: Association Press, 1958.

Kainen, Ruth Cole. *America's Christmas Heritage*. New York: Funk & Wagnalls, 1969.

Krythe, Mamie. *All About Christmas*. New York: Harper & Brothers, 1954.

Listaite, Gratia. *New Look at Christmas Decorations*. Milwaukee: Bruce Publications, 1957.

Metcalfe, Edna. *The Trees of Christmas*. Nashville: Abingdon, 1969.

Newsome, Arden. *Crafts and Toys from Around the World*. New York: Julian Messner, 1972.

Nold, Liselotte. *Cradling the Christ Child*. Minneapolis: Augsburg Publishing House, 1965.

Payne, Alma. *Jingle Bells and Pastry Shells*. Cleveland: World Publishing Company, 1968.

Perry, Margaret. *Christmas Card Magic*. Garden City, N.Y.: Doubleday & Co., 1967.

Polanie Publishing Company Staff. *Treasured Polish Christmas Customs and Traditions*. Minneapolis: Polanie Publishing Co., 1972.

Christmas Crafts For Everyone

Purdy, Susan. *Christmas Decorations for You to Make.* Philadelphia: J. B. Lippincott Co., 1965.

Sheraton, Mimi. *Visions of Sugarplums.* New York: Random House, 1968.

Trapp, Maria. *Around the Year with The Trapp Family.* New York: Pantheon Books, 1955.

Waugh, Dorothy. *A Handbook of Christmas Decorations.* New York: Macmillan Co., 1958.

Weiser, Francis X. *The Christmas Book.* New York: Harcourt Brace Jovanovich, 1952.

INDEX

Entries in **boldface type** indicate illustrations.

143